Audio Tape Program

Audio Tape Program

A Workbook

Anne Lindell

Ann Arbor   The University of Michigan Press

Copyright © by The University of Michigan 1983
All rights reserved
ISBN 0-472-08573-5
Library of Congress Catalog Card No. 83-50326
Published in the United States of America by
The University of Michigan Press
Manufactured in the United States of America

1991   7 6 5

Acknowledgments

The recording and production of the tape program for *Audio Tape Program: A Workbook* would not have been possible without the voices of Daniel Bilodeau, Fay Radding, and Alan Willoughby, nor the tireless effort of James L. Bixler, broadcast engineer, who recorded the entire script. To all of them I give my sincere thanks. I would also like to express my appreciation to James O. Yzenbaard, director of the Language Laboratory of the University of Michigan for his support of this project.

Contents

Introduction 1

Lesson 1: Asking for Information 3
    Conversation   3
    Vocabulary Focus: Names; Titles of Address; Formal and Informal Introductions   4
    Let's Practice I—Present Continuous Tense   4
    Let's Practice II—Simple Present Tense   5
    Let's Practice III—Present Perfect Tense (Part 1)   6

Lesson 2: Reporting the Facts 8
    Conversation   8
    Vocabulary Focus: Banking Terms; The Verbs *Borrow* and *Lend*   9
    Let's Practice I—Simple Past Tense   10
    Let's Practice II—Past Continuous Tense   11
    Let's Practice III—Emphatic *Do, Does, Did*   12
    Let's Practice IV—The Passive Voice (Part 1)   12

Lesson 3: What's the Weather Like? 14
    Conversation   14
    Vocabulary Focus: Weather and Climate Expressions; Listening Comprehension;
        The Climate of North America Continued   15
    Let's Practice I—Single-Word Adverbs of Frequency   15
    Let's Practice II—*How Often* and *How Long*   16
    Let's Practice III—*There Is* and *There Are*   17
    Let's Practice IV—Future Time   18

Lesson 4: Have You Heard the News? 20
    Conversation   20
    Vocabulary Focus: *Have Got*   20
    Let's Practice I—Relative Clauses (Part 1)   20
    Let's Practice II—Present Perfect Tense (Part 2)   21
    Let's Practice III—Time Expressions Used with the Present Perfect and
        Simple Past Tenses   22

Lesson 5: Aches and Pains 23
    Conversation   23
    Vocabulary Focus: Expressions of Aches and Pains; Being Sick or Injured;
        What does a doctor do? What does a nurse do?; True or False?   23
    Let's Practice I—Noun Modifiers   24
    Let's Practice II—Adverbs of Manner   26
    Let's Practice III—Word Order in Sentences   26

Lesson 6: Making Comparisons 28
    Vocabulary Focus: Verbs of Sight: *See, Look At, Watch, Stare,* and *Observe*   28
    Let's Practice I—Comparison of Adjectives and Adverbs: Comparative and
        Superlative Degrees   28

Contents

    Let's Practice II—Expressions of Equality, Similarity, and Difference:
        As, The Same As, Like, and *Different From*   29
    Let's Practice III—Expressions of Quantity (Part 1): Count and Noncount Nouns   30
    Let's Practice IV—Expressions of Quantity (Part 2): *A Lot Of, A Little, A Few,*
        Enough, Many, and *Much*   31

Lesson 7: Houses and Apartments 33
    Conversation   33
    Vocabulary Focus: Rooms of the House and Furniture   33
    Let's Practice I—Expressions of Place: *In, At, On*   34
    Let's Practice II—The Definite Article: *The*   34
    Let's Practice III—Comparison of Nouns: Comparative and Superlative Degrees   36
    Let's Practice IV—Demonstrative Adjectives and Pronouns: *This, These,*
        That, and *Those*   36

Lesson 8: Making Requests and Complaints 38
    Conversation   38
    Vocabulary Focus: The Verb *Get; Be Used To, Get Used To*   38
    Let's Practice I—Requests and Suggestions   39
    Let's Practice II—Adverbs of Intensification: *Very, Too, Much,* and *Enough*   40
    Let's Practice III—Indefinite Expressions: *Someone, No One, Anyone*   41
    Let's Practice IV—Elliptical Verb Forms   42

Lesson 9: Necessity and Obligation 43
    Conversation   43
    Vocabulary Focus: The Verb *Take*   43
    Let's Practice I—Expressions of Necessity: *Must, Have To, Be Required To*   44
    Let's Practice II—Expressions of Obligation: *Should, Ought To, Had Better,* and
        Be Supposed To   44
    Let's Practice III—Past of Modal Auxiliary Verbs (Part 1): *Must Have* and
        Should Have   45
    Let's Practice IV—*Both* and *Each, Either . . . Or,* and *Neither . . . Nor*   47

Lesson 10: Can You Drive a Car? 49
    Conversation   49
    Vocabulary Focus: Parts of the Car   49
    Let's Practice I—Expressions of Ability: *Can, Could,* and *Be Able*   49
    Let's Practice II—Expressions of Permission: *May, Can, Allow, Let,* and *Be Allowed To*   50
    Let's Practice III—Making Questions by Rising Intonation   52
    Let's Practice IV—Tag Questions   52

Lesson 11: Looking for a Job 54
    Conversation   54
    Vocabulary Focus: Occupations   54
    Let's Practice I—Expressions of Possibility: *May, Might, Can, Could,* and
        It's Possible That   55
    Let's Practice II—Past of Modal Auxiliary Verbs (Part 2): *May Have,*
        Might Have, and *Could Have*   55
    Let's Practice III—Past Perfect Tense and Future Perfect Tense   57
    Let's Practice IV—Subordinating Conjunctions: *Before* and *After*   57

Lesson 12: On the Road 59
    Conversation   59
    Vocabulary Focus: Indefinite *You, They,* and *One;* The Verbs *Make* and *Do*   59
    Let's Practice I—Conditional Clauses with *If* (Part 1): Present   60
    Let's Practice II—Conditional Clauses with *Unless* and Conditional Clauses
       with *If* (Part 2): Past   61
    Let's Practice III—Reported Speech and Indirect Questions   62
    Let's Practice IV—Possessive Nouns   63

Lesson 13: Writing a Letter 64
    Conversation   64
    Vocabulary Focus: The Verbs *Say, Tell, Speak,* and *Talk*   64
    Let's Practice I—Verbals: Infinitives   65
    Let's Practice II—Gerunds   66
    Let's Practice III—Verbs That Take a Noun Followed by the Infinitive and Verbs and
       Adjectives of Desire, Necessity, and Urgency Followed by a Noun Clause   67
    Let's Practice IV—Verbs Followed by a Noun and a Gerund and Verbs Followed
       by a Noun with a Preposition and a Gerund   68

Lesson 14: Sports and Recreation 69
    Conversation   69
    Vocabulary Focus: Sports and Recreational Activities   70
    Let's Practice I—Expressions of Preference: *Would Rather, Prefer,* and *Like Better*   70
    Let's Practice II—Verbs with Inseparable Particles, Verbs with Separable Particles,
       and Verbs Plus a Preposition   71
    Let's Practice III—Expressions of Cause and Effect and Expressions of Contrast   72
    Let's Practice IV—Result Clauses and *Whether or Not*   75

Lesson 15: Education and Future Plans 76
    Conversation   76
    Vocabulary Focus: Educational Institutions in the United States   76
    Let's Practice I—Expressions with Verbs and Adjectives That Take
       Particles and/or Prepositions   77
    Let's Practice II—The Verb *Wish*   78
    Let's Practice III—Present and Past Participles as Adjectives and Past Participles
       as Adjective Complement after the Direct Object   79
    Let's Practice IV—The Passive Voice (Part 2) and Sentence Connectors:
       Moreover, However, Therefore   80

Tape Script 83

Introduction

Audio Tape Program is a workbook containing the exercises (also available on cassette) for all fifteen lessons of the textbook *Intensive English for Communication: Book 2*. Each lesson of the workbook corresponds to the same lesson of the textbook. Supplementary aural-oral exercises are also included. The cassette tapes may be ordered directly from the University of Michigan Press.[1]

Audio Tape Program may be used separately from the text, however, for intermediate students as a kind of general review and practice of basic English grammar emphasizing listening and speaking skills. In this case, either the students should have access to the textbook itself to study the grammar explanations and examples, or the teacher will have to provide the rules and illustrations for each part of the lesson. A list of all the language structures that are included can be found on the contents page.

The recorded exercises include such activities as listening to and repeating dialogues, vocabulary items, and grammatical patterns; answering questions and making transformations of various structures; writing responses in the workbook to oral questions heard on the tape; listening to a passage and then answering questions either verbally or in writing; answering true/false and multiple choice questions by circling the appropriate choice in the workbook; responding to visual cues, such as pictures or maps; and writing dictations of several sentences in every lesson. Most of the exercises come from *Intensive English for Communication: Book 2*; however, not all of the exercises from that book have been included, and there are some additional ones written solely for the workbook.

The students follow the recorded exercises in their workbook. The topic of each exercise or activity, the directions indicating the type of response to be given, and the example, are all printed for the students so they should be able to understand what they have to do without resorting to the tape script. The tape script with the correct answers for all oral and written responses and the dictations is included at the end of the workbook. For some of the longer exercises, of course, students may want to look at the tape script first and then try the exercises.

As the students follow the examples given in their workbook, they will see numbers printed horizontally across the page. These numbers indicate the number of items they will hear on the tape, enabling them to keep track of where they are. Here is a sample of the format of the workbook, taken from page 5.

Let's Practice II—Simple Present Tense

A. *Listen to the sentences in the simple present tense.*
Listen for the final -s at the end of third person singular verbs.

1 2 3 4 5 6

Now repeat the sentences after the speaker.

1 2 3 4 5 6

There are ample pauses on the tape for students to respond after the cue has been given. The correct answer is then provided with yet another pause for repetition by the students.

---

1. University of Michigan Press, P.O. Box 1104, 839 Greene Street, Ann Arbor, Michigan, 48106; phone: 313-764-4392.

Introduction

The exercises which call for written responses are to be completed in the space provided in the workbook.

Lesson 1
Asking for Information

(Listen to the exercises that you hear on the tape as you follow along in your workbook. Try to do all the exercises at least once before looking at the tape script for lesson 1, which is found on page 83.)

Conversation

Questions and Answers. *These are typical questions asked of foreign students. First listen to the conversation between Mrs. Foster and Ali.*

Mrs. Foster:
Ali:

Now pretend that you are answering Mrs. Foster. Tell her about yourself. Do not give Ali's answers. You will hear each question twice. Answer in the pause that follows.

1   2   3   4

Listen to the next part of the conversation.

Mrs. Foster:
Ali:

Now answer the questions. Tell about yourself.

1   2   3

Listen to the next part of the conversation.

Mrs. Foster:
Ali:

Now answer the questions. Tell about yourself.

1   2   3

Listen to the rest of the conversation.

Mrs. Foster:
Ali:

Now answer the questions. Tell about yourself.

1   2   3

Lesson 1

Vocabulary Focus

1. Names
   Listen to the following conversation. You will hear it twice in succession.

   Answer the question in the pause provided. The correct answer will be given after the pause.

   1 2 3 4 5 6

2. Titles of Address
   Listen, read, and repeat the following names with their titles of address. Each item will be heard twice in succession.

   Mr. Fraser, Mr. Schwartz, Ms. Peterson, Ms. Chang, Mrs. Hanson, Mrs. Gomez, Miss Wilson, Miss Park, Dr. Sato, Dr. Haddad

3. Formal and Informal Introductions
   Listen to the conversation. It is a formal introduction.

   Now repeat the dialogue after the speaker.

   Listen to the next conversation. It is an informal introduction.

   Now repeat the dialogue.

   Listen to the conversation. It's a formal greeting.

   Now repeat the dialogue after the speaker.

   Listen to the informal greeting.

   Now repeat the dialogue.

Let's Practice I—Present Continuous Tense

A. *Listen to the short passage and then answer the questions. The passage will be heard twice in succession.*

Answer the questions in the pause provided. The correct answer will be given after the pause.

1 2 3 4 5 6 7 8

B. *Listen to the two verbs and make affirmative and negative sentences in the present continuous tense. Use the pronoun* I *as the subject. First look at and listen to the example in your workbook.*

Example: work walk. **I'm working. I'm not walking.**

1 2 3 4 5 6

C. *Now repeat the exercise and use* you *as the subject.*

   Example: work   walk. **You're working. You aren't walking.**

   1   2   3   4   5   6

D. *Do the same exercise using* he *as the subject.*

   Example: work   walk. **He's working. He isn't walking.**

   1   2   3   4   5   6

E. *Read the sentences in your workbook as you listen to the speaker. These sentences are answers to questions. Ask the question that goes to these answers in the pause provided. Use the question word given in parentheses. You will hear the correct answer after the pause.*

   Example: I'm looking for *the post office*. (What)
   What are you looking for?

   1. I'm asking the policeman *a question*. (What)
   2. I'm going *to the bank* later. (Where)
   3. I'm thinking about *something*. (What)
   4. My friend is arriving *next Thursday*. (When)
   5. Henry is talking to *someone*. (Who)
   6. The students are paying *a lot of* money for this course. (How much)
   7. We're leaving *at six o'clock*. (What time)
   8. They're buying a bigger house *because they need more space*. (Why)

Let's Practice II—Simple Present Tense

A. *Listen to the sentences in the simple present tense. Listen for the final* -s *at the end of third person singular verbs.*

   1   2   3   4   5   6

   Now repeat the sentences after the speaker.

   1   2   3   4   5   6

B. *Listen to these negative statements and questions. Listen carefully to the negative auxiliary* don't—doesn't *and the question auxiliary* do—does.

   1   2   3   4   5   6   7   8   9   10   11   12

   Now repeat the sentences after the speaker.

   1   2   3   4   5   6   7   8   9   10   11

Lesson 1

C. What does a good student do? *Tell what a good student does and doesn't do from this list of phrases. There will be a pause for you to respond and then the correct answer will be given. First listen to the example.*

Example: study hard. **A good student studies hard.**
go to bed late every night. **A good student doesn't go to bed late every night.**

1 2 3 4 5 6 7 8

Let's Practice III—Present Perfect Tense (Part 1)

A. *Listen to the sentences in the present perfect.*

1 2 3 4 5 6 7 8

Now repeat the sentences after the speaker.

1 2 3 4 5 6 7 8

B. *Listen to the sentences in the present perfect continuous.*

1 2 3 4 5 6

Now repeat the sentences after the speaker.

1 2 3 4 5 6

C. *Listen to the questions and answers with* **how long.**

1 2 3 4 5 6

Now repeat the questions and answers after the speaker. Each sentence will be given only once.

1 2 3 4 5 6

D. Listening-Writing Response. *Listen to the questions and write the answers in your workbook. Tell about yourself. You will hear each question twice. Then write the answer.*

1. _____
2. _____
3. _____
4. _____

Lesson 1

E. **Dictation.** *Listen and write the sentences. Each sentence will be read three times. Listen to the sentence the first time. Then write the sentence after the second time. Check your written sentence after the third time. Note that one of the sentences is a question.*

1. _____
2. _____
3. _____
4. _____

Lesson 2
Reporting the Facts

(Listen to the exercises that you hear on the tape as you follow along in your workbook. Try to do all the exercises at least once before looking at the tape script for lesson 2, which is found on page 88.)

Conversation

A. **The Great Bank Robbery.** *Listen to the introduction and then the conversation between the newspaper reporter and Miss Lee.*

> There was a big commotion on Main Street yesterday. Sirens were blaring, people were screaming, and a policeman was holding up traffic. A newspaper reporter stopped a young woman. She was running down the street.

Reporter:
Miss Lee:

B. **Listening-Writing Response.** *You will hear this conversation again. In your workbook write the question that you hear the reporter ask. There will be a pause for you to fill in the correct response. Then read Miss Lee's answer along with the speaker. The first one is done for you.*

Example: *Reporter:* <u>What happened?</u>

   Miss Lee: The bank was robbed.

Reporter: _____

Miss Lee: First National Bank.

Reporter: _____

Miss Lee: About fifteen minutes ago.

Reporter: _____

Miss Lee: I don't know. A bad guy. He was wearing a mask.

Reporter: _____

Miss Lee: He threatened the teller with a gun.

Reporter: _____

Miss Lee: He escaped through the back door.

Reporter: _____

Lesson 2

Miss Lee: Someone said over a hundred thousand dollars.

Reporter: _____

Miss Lee: I don't think so, but the thief fired two shots into the air before he left.

Vocabulary Focus

1. Banking Terms
   Look at the list of words in your workbook and repeat them after the speaker. The definitions for these terms are given on page 16 of Intensive English for Communication: Book 2. *You will hear each item only once.*

Nouns	Verbs
checking account	borrow
checkbook	lend
check	deposit money
traveler's check	withdraw money
savings accounts	
savings passbook	
loan	
debt	
interest	

   The Verbs *borrow* and *lend*

A. *Listen to these sentences with* borrow.

   1 2 3 4 5 6 7

   Now repeat the sentences after the speaker. Each sentence will be heard twice in succession.

   1 2 3 4 5 6 7

B. *Listen to these sentences with* lend.

   1 2 3 4 5 6 7

   Now repeat the sentences after the speaker. Each sentence will be heard twice in succession.

   1 2 3 4 5 6 7

Lesson 2

C. ***Borrow* versus *Lend*.** *Listen to the following sentences with* borrow *and* lend. *Only one of the words—*borrow *or* lend*—is correct in each case. In your workbook put a circle around the correct word. Each sentence will be read twice.*

Example: I don't have enough money for the show. I will have to (borrow) lend some.

Borrow *is the correct choice.* Borrow *is circled in your workbook.*

1. borrow   lend
2. borrowed   lent
3. borrow   lend
4. borrow   lend

5. borrowed   lent
6. borrow   lend
7. borrow   lend
   borrow   lend

Let's Practice I—Simple Past Tense

A. **Regular Verbs.** *Look at the verbs and sentences in your workbook and repeat them after the speaker.*

1. I looked. I looked at page six.
2. I watched. I watched TV last night.
3. We stopped. We stopped at the traffic light.
4. We studied. We studied hard last night.
5. You played. You played chess with me last year.
6. You borrowed. Remember, you borrowed twenty dollars from me.
7. Bob smiled. Bob smiled at us.
8. He wanted something. He wanted to talk to us.
9. He needed. He needed some information.
10. Mary decided. Mary decided to go to New York.

B. *Now repeat these sentences in the negative.*

1. I didn't look at page six.
2. I didn't watch TV last night.
3. We didn't stop at the traffic light.
4. We didn't study hard last night.
5. You didn't play chess with me last year.
6. Bob didn't need any information.

C. **Irregular Verbs.** *Look at these verbs in the present and past tense and repeat them after the speaker.*

1. I see. I saw.
2. I spend. I spent.
3. We make. We made.
4. We give. We gave.
5. Bill eats. He ate.
6. He speaks. He spoke.
7. Sue reads. She read.
8. She gets. She got.
9. They think. They thought.
10. They go. They went.

11. You do. You did.
12. You come. You came.
13. He leaves. He left.
14. He knows. He knew.
15. I write. I wrote.
16. I sleep. I slept.
17. She lends. She lent.
18. She takes. She took.
19. We teach. We taught.
20. We drink. We drank.

Lesson 2

D. *Listen to the sentences. Then write the verbs in the answer blanks as you listen to the sentence again. The verbs may be either affirmative or negative. You will hear each sentence two times.*

Example: I *saw* Jack yesterday, but I *didn't see* Paul.

Now write the verb saw *in the first blank space, and write* didn't see *in the second blank space.*

_____ _____

1. _____ _____

2. _____ _____

3. _____ _____ _____

4. _____ _____

5. _____ _____ _____

E. **Questions.** *Listen to the statements and the question word that is given. They will be heard twice in succession. In the pause provided ask a question using the question word. Use* you *as the subject.*

Example: I did something yesterday. What?
What did you do?

1 2 3 4 5 6

Let's Practice II—Past Continuous Tense

A. **Answering Questions.** *Answer these questions in the past continuous tense by using the verb or expression that you hear after the question.*

Examples: What were you doing last night? watch TV
I was watching TV last night.
Where was John going yesterday? to the store
He was going to the store.

1 2 3 4 5 6

B. **Listening Comprehension.** *Listen to the passage and the eight questions that follow. Do not answer the questions the first time. You will hear the same passage and the questions a second time. Answer the questions in the pause provided.*

1 2 3 4 5 6 7 8

C. **Used To.** *Listen to these dialogues with* used to.

1 2 3 4 5

Lesson 2

D. Listening-Writing Response. *You will hear the same questions with* used to. *This time write answers about yourself and your own family in your workbook. Each question will be heard two times.*

1. _____

2. _____

3. _____

4. _____

5. _____

Let's Practice III—Emphatic *Do, Does, Did*

Indeed I do. *Answer the questions by using the appropriate auxiliary verb,* do, does, *or* did *in an affirmative statement.* Indeed *means* certainly *or* definitely.

Example: Do you miss your country?
Yes, indeed. I *do* miss my country.

1 2 3 4 5 6

Let's Practice IV—The Passive Voice (Part 1)

A. *Read the incomplete dialogue in your workbook while listening to the complete conversation that you hear on the tape. Then go back to number 1 and fill in the missing lines with the correct response.*

Example: Why was the traffic held up on Main Street yesterday?
The traffic was held up on Main Street because *the bank was robbed.*

1. Which bank was robbed?

   First National Bank _____

2. What time was it robbed?

   It _____ in the morning.

3. How much money was stolen?

   Over one hundred thousand dollars _____

4. How was the teller threatened?

   The teller _____ with a gun.

Lesson 2

5. How many shots were fired?

   _____

6. Was the teller killed?

   No, _____

7. Was anyone hurt?

   No, _____

8. What time was the robbery reported to the police?

   The robbery _____

B. *Answer these questions in the passive voice. Each question will be heard two times.*

   Example: Where are kangaroos found?
   Kangaroos are found in Australia.

   1 2 3 4 5 6 7 8 9 10 11 12

C. **Dictation.** *Listen and write the sentences. Each sentence will be read three times. Listen to the sentence the first time. Then write the sentence after the second time. Check your written sentence after the third time.*

   1. _____

   2. _____

   3. _____

Lesson 3
What's the Weather Like?

(Listen to the exercises that you hear on the tape as you follow along in your workbook. Try to do all the exercises at least once before looking at the tape script for lesson 3, which is found on page 93.)

Conversation

What Season Is It? *Look at the pictures and listen to the sentences. Repeat the sentences after the speaker.*

Spring

Winter

Summer

Fall

1 2 3 4

Lesson 3

Vocabulary Focus

A. Weather and Climate Expressions
    Listen to these expressions pertaining to weather and climate. Repeat them after the speaker. These words are found on page 34 of Intensive English for Communication: Book 2.

B. Listening Comprehension
    Listen to the passage about the climate of North America and the five questions that follow. Do not answer the questions the first time. You will hear the same passage and the questions a second time. Answer the questions in the pause provided.

    1 2 3 4 5

C. The Climate of North America Continued
    Listen to the rest of the passage and the questions. There are five questions in this part.

    1 2 3 4 5

Let's Practice I—Single-Word Adverbs of Frequency

A. *Look at the map of the United States and listen to the sentences. Repeat the sentences after the speaker.*

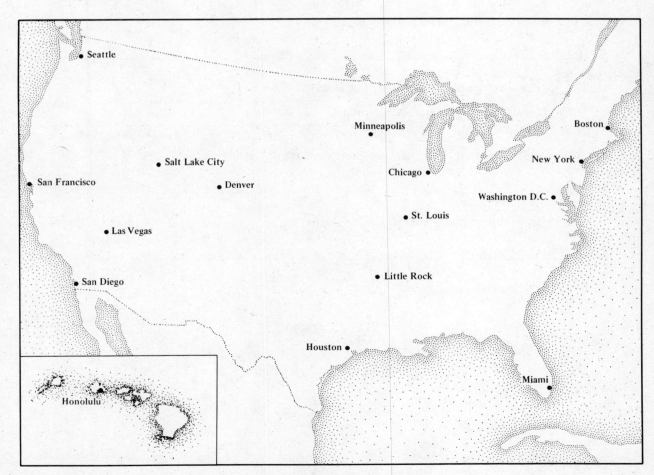

1 2 3 4 5 6 7 8 9 10

Lesson 3

B. *Look at the map of the United States and answer these questions in complete sentences using the adverb of frequency that is given.*

   Example: Does it always snow in San Diego in December? No, never
   No, it never snows in San Diego in December.

   1 2 3 4 5 6 7 8

Let's Practice II—*How Often* and *How Long*

A. *Listen to these conversations.*

   1 2 3 4 5 6

B. **Listening-Writing Response.** *You will hear this conversation again. In your workbook write the question that you hear the speaker ask. The first one is done for you.*

   1. *How often do you see Bob?*

   I see him once a month.

   2. _____

   I usually play tennis three times a week.

   3. _____

   The mail comes once a day, five days a week.

   4. _____

   School lasts from eight in the morning to three in the afternoon.

   5. _____

   I've been here for three years.

   6. _____

   It will last approximately two hours.

C. **Richard's Schedule.** *Look at Richard's schedule and answer the questions.*

DAY / HOUR	Mon.	Tues.	Wed.	Thurs.	Fri.
9	French	French	French	French	Library
10	Chem. Lecture	Lang. Lab.	Chem. Lecture	Lang. Lab	Chem. Lecture
11	Econ.	Library	Econ.	Library	Econ.
12	English	Lunch	English	Lunch	English
1	Lunch	Library	Lunch	Library	Lunch
2	Library	Chem. Lab	Phys. Ed.	Chem. Lab	Phys. Ed.
3	Library	Chem. Lab	Phys. Ed.	Chem. Lab	Phys. Ed.

1 2 3 4 5 6 7 8

Let's Practice III—*There Is* and *There Are*

A. *Listen to the sentences and restate them using* there is *or* there are. *In the past tense use* there was *and* there were.

   Examples: A good movie is on TV tonight.
   There's a good movie on TV tonight.
   Old movies were playing on TV.
   There were old movies playing on TV.

1 2 3 4 5 6

B. *Listen to these negative sentences with* there isn't *and* there aren't. *Then give the alternate form,* there is no *and* there are no, *in the pause provided.*

   Examples: There aren't any seats left in the theater.
   There are no seats left in the theater.
   There isn't any money on the table.
   There is no money on the table.

1 2 3 4 5 6 7 8

Lesson 3

Let's Practice IV—Future Time

A. **Listening Comprehension.** *Listen to the passage about plans for the summer and the questions that follow. Do not answer the questions the first time. You will hear the same passage and the questions a second time. Answer the questions in the pause provided. There are five questions in this part.*

   1 2 3 4 5

B. **Plans for the Summer Continued**

   1 2 3 4 5

C. **Questions with *Be Going To*.** *Use the verb expression and the question word that you hear and make up a question with* be going to.

   Example: listen to the radio; when
   When are you going to listen to the radio?

   1 2 3 4 5 6

D. **Questions with *Will*.** *Repeat exercise C using* will *instead of* be going to.

   Example: live next year; where
   Where will you live next year?

   1 2 3 4 5 6

E. **Promises.** *Make a promise using* will. *Change the sentences according to the example. Use the contraction form of* will.

   Example: I promise to be there on time.
   I'll be there on time.

   1 2 3 4 5 6

F. **Listening-Writing Response.** *Listen to the weather forecasts and then answer the questions in writing in your workbook. Use short answers,* Yes, it will *or* No, it won't. *The forecasts and questions will be heard twice in succession.*

   1. _____

   2. _____

   3. _____

   4. _____

18

1. _____
2. _____
3. _____
4. _____

G. **Dictation.** *Listen and write the sentences. Each sentence will be read three times. Listen to the sentence the first time. Then write the sentence after the second time. Check your written sentence after the third time.*

1. _____
2. _____
3. _____

Lesson 4
Have You Heard the News?

(Listen to the exercises that you hear on the tape as you follow along in your workbook. Try to do all the exercises at least once before looking at the tape script for lesson 4, which is found on page 99.)

Conversation

   A. **The Latest Gossip.** *Listen to the conversation.*

     Kathy:
     Phil:

     Now repeat the sentences after the speaker.

     Kathy:
     Phil:

   B. **I'm sorry to hear about it.** *Listen to the next conversation.*

     Tom:
     Julie:

     Now repeat the sentences after the speaker.

     Tom:
     Julie:

Vocabulary Focus

   Have Got

A. *Listen to the sentences. Each sentence will be given twice. The first time you will hear the full form with* have *or* has. *The second time you will hear the contraction. Repeat both sentences after the speaker.*

    1 2 3 4 5 6 7

B. *Listen to the questions and answers. Then you will hear the question again and a pause for you to give the answer. The correct response will be given again after the pause.*

    1 2 3 4 5 6

Let's Practice I—Relative Clauses (Part 1)

   A. *Listen to the two sentences and then combine them with the relative pronoun that is given.*

Lesson 4

Example: I see the boy. The boy is happy. who
I see the boy who is happy.

1 2 3 4 5 6

B. *Combine the two sentences by putting the relative clause in the middle of the main clause.*

Example: The girl broke her leg. She has to walk on crutches. who
The girl who broke her leg has to walk on crutches.

1 2 3 4

C. *Combine the two sentences with the possessive relative pronoun* whose.

Example: I see the boy. His dog is lost.
I see the boy whose dog is lost.

1 2 3 4 5

Let's Practice II—Present Perfect Tense (Part 2)

A. **Contractions.** *Listen to the sentences in the present perfect and repeat the sentences using the contraction.*

1 2 3 4 5 6 7 8 9 10

B. **Present Perfect Continuous.** *Listen to the questions and answers.*

1 2 3 4 5

C. **Listening-Writing Response.** *Listen to the same questions and answers. Then you will hear the question again with a pause. During the pause write the correct response in your workbook.*

1. _____
2. _____
3. _____
4. _____
5. _____

D. **Asking Questions.** *Listen to the sentences and ask a question using the question word given.*

Example: Tommy has been crying all day. why
Why has Tommy been crying all day?

1 2 3 4 5 6

Lesson 4

Let's Practice III—Time Expressions Used with the Present Perfect and Simple Past Tenses

A. **Listening Comprehension.** *Listen to the situations and then answer the questions in the pause provided. You will hear each situation twice.*

   1   2   3   4

B. *Since* **and** *For.* *Answer the questions with a complete sentence using the phrase that is given with* since *or* for.

   Example: How long have you lived in this country? since September
   I've lived in this country since September.

   1   2   3   4   5   6

C. *Already.* *Answer the questions using* already *and the correct form of the verb that is given.*

   Example: Did you start your homework yet? finish
   I've already finished my homework.

   1   2   3   4   5   6

D. *Yet.* *Make up questions with* yet *by using the present perfect tense of the verb phrase given. Use* you *as the subject.*

   Example: see John
   Have you seen John yet?

   1   2   3   4   5   6   7   8

E. **Summary Practice.** *Review short answer forms for all verb tenses. Answer the questions using the appropriate short answer. Yes* or *no will be given for you.*

   Example: Are you studying English now? yes
   Yes, I am.

   1   2   3   4   5   6   7   8   9   10   11   12   13   14   15

F. **Dictation.** *Listen and write the sentences. Each sentence will be read three times. Listen to the sentence the first time. Then write the sentence after the second time. Check your written sentence after the third time.*

   1. _____
   2. _____
   3. _____
   4. _____

Lesson 5
Aches and Pains

(Listen to the exercises that you hear on the tape as you follow along in your workbook. Try to do all the exercises at least once before looking at the tape script for lesson 5, which is found on page 104.)

Conversation

A. At the Doctor's. *Listen to the conversation.*

Doctor:
Patient:

Now repeat the sentences after the speaker.

Doctor:
Patient:

B. Where does it Hurt? *Listen to the next conversation.*

Doctor:
Patient:

Now repeat the sentences after the speaker.

Doctor:
Patient:

Vocabulary Focus

1. Expressions of Aches and Pains
   Listen to the sentences with ache *and* sore *and repeat them after the speaker. These expressions are found on page 71 of* Intensive English for Communication: Book 2.

   1 2 3 4 5 6 7 8 9 10

2. Being Sick or Injured
   Listen and repeat these expressions of illness and injury. They are also found on pages 71 and 72 of Book 2.

   1 2 3 4 5 6 7 8 9 10 11 12 13 14 15 16 17 18 19 20 21 22
   23 24 25 26 27 28 29 30

3. What does a doctor do? What does a nurse do?
   Listen and repeat the sentences. These sentences are found on page 72 of Book 2.

   1 2 3 4 5 6 7 8 9 10 11

Lesson 5

4. True or False

   Listen to the statements. If the statement is correct, circle true *in your workbook. If the statement is not correct, circle* false. *Each sentence will be heard twice in succession.*

   Examples: 1. If you have a bad cold, you should stay home and rest.   True   False

   The answer is true. Circle true *in your workbook.*

   2. If you are shivering you should take your sweater off.   True   False

   The answer is false. Circle false *in your workbook.*

   1. True   False
   2. True   False
   3. True   False
   4. True   False
   5. True   False
   6. True   False
   7. True   False
   8. True   False

Let's Practice I—Noun Modifiers

A. **Adjectives.** *Listen to the two sentences and then combine them by using the adjective in the second sentence to describe the noun in the first sentence.*

   Example: The woman is Dr. Peterson's wife. She is tall and slender.
   The tall slender woman is Dr. Peterson's wife.

   1 2 3 4 5 6

B. **Prepositional Phrases.** *Combine the two sentences by using the prepositional phrase in the second sentence to describe the noun in the first sentence.*

   Example: The surgeon operated on me. The surgeon was from Canada.
   The surgeon from Canada operated on me.

   1 2 3 4 5 6

C. **Present and Past Participial Phrases.** *Combine the two sentences by using the present or past participle in the second sentence to describe the noun in the first sentence.*

   Examples: The woman wants to go to the station. She is waiting for a taxi.
   The woman waiting for a taxi wants to go to the station.
   We looked everywhere for the keys. They were lost.
   We looked everywhere for the lost keys.

   1 2 3 4 5 6

D. **Relative Clauses (Part 2): Relative Pronoun in Object Position.** *Combine these sentences using a relative clause. In this exercise use* whom *for a person and* which *for a thing.*

Examples: Here comes the bus. We are taking it.
Here comes the bus which we are taking.
I would like you to meet my friend. You don't know him.
I would like you to meet my friend whom you don't know.

1 2 3 4 5 6

E. Relative Pronoun: *Whose*. *Combine these sentences using the relative pronoun* whose.

Example: There is the professor. We know his wife.
There is the professor whose wife we know.

1 2 3 4 5 6

F. Relative Clauses with *Where* and *When*. *Combine these sentences by using* where *or* when *to introduce the relative clause.*

Examples: This is the town. I was born there.
This is the town where I was born.
I know the day. I was born on that day.
I know the day when I was born.

1 2 3 4 5 6

G. Listening-Reading Response: True/False. *Listen to the sentences. In your workbook read the two responses for each sentence. If the response is correct according to the sentence you heard on the tape, circle* T *in the answer column. If the answer is not correct, circle* F *in the answer column. You will hear each sentence twice.*

Example: Last Thursday was the day when the team, still coached by Teddy Robinson, lost its first game.

Now read to yourself sentences a *and* b *in your workbook and decide if they are true or false.*

    a. Until last Thursday the team used to win all its games.   T   F

    b. Last Thursday was the first game played that was coached by Teddy Robinson.   T   F

Sentence a *is true. Circle* T *in the answer column.*
Sentence b *is false. Circle* F *in the answer column.*

Ready? Begin.

1. a. Bob needs to have an operation on his knee.   T   F

   b. Bob knows the doctor who will operate on him.   T   F

2. a. I was born in a good-sized village.   T   F

   b. I was born in a village which didn't have very many people living in it.   T   F

Lesson 5

    3. a. Steve had the same teacher whom his friend had for computer science.   T F

       b. Steve's friend took a computer science course.   T F

    4. a. The boy's dog was judged to be the best dog in the dog show.   T F

       b. The boy was an excellent math student.   T F

    5. a. Mary had to return to France.   T F

       b. The French soldier was not in his own country when Mary fell in love with him.   T F

    6. a. Dr. Kelsey's son just wrecked the family car.   T F

       b. Dr. Kelsey's good friend just wrecked the family car.   T F

Let's Practice II—Adverbs of Manner

A. *Listen to the sentences with the verb* be *followed by an adjective. Then a new verb will be given. Make up a new sentence using the same subject with the new verb. Change the adjective of the first sentence to its corresponding adverb. Look at the examples in your workbook.*

    Examples: Jack is nervous. is behaving
                    Jack is behaving nervously.
                    The children were high in the tree. climbed
                    The children climbed high in the tree.

    1 2 3 4 5 6 7 8 9 10 11 12

B. *Answer the questions in a complete sentence. You will hear each question twice.*

    Example: Do good drivers drive recklessly or carefully?
                    Good drivers drive carefully.

    1 2 3 4 5 6 7

Let's Practice III—Word Order in Sentences

A. Subject—Verb—Object. *Listen to these sentences as you read them in your workbook. Write* S *for subject,* V *for verb, and* O *for object, above the words in your workbook.*

                   S   V   O
    Example: Mary threw the ball.

Mary is the subject of the sentence. Therefore, write an S *above the word* Mary. Threw *is the verb. Write a* V *above the word* threw. The ball *is the object. Write an* O *above the words* the ball. *Continue the exercise.*

1. The train left.

2. It was raining.

3. The cat caught a mouse.

4. Tom will write a letter.

5. We can't forget our passports.

6. The students were playing soccer.

B. **Expressions of Place and Time.** *Listen to the position of expressions of place and time in these sentences. Write* time *or* place *above the appropriate words for each sentence in your workbook.*

Example: Barbara goes to the gym every day.

Write place *above the words* to the gym *and* time *above the words* every day.

1. My friends drove to Tennessee last Friday.

2. The teacher read the announcement in class yesterday.

3. The students go to the library at four o'clock every afternoon.

4. We ate at a good restaurant last week.

C. **Direct and Indirect Objects.** *Certain verbs which take a direct object may also take an indirect object. Listen to these sentences as you read them in your workbook. Write* direct *and* indirect *above the direct and indirect object for each sentence in your workbook.*

Example: Mother made sandwiches for everyone.

1. Ted gave roses to his girlfriend.

2. I got a hotel room for Linda and Susan.

3. I mailed a letter to Bob.

4. Tom did a big favor for me.

D. **Indirect Object before the Direct Object.** *With certain verbs the indirect object precedes the direct object when the preposition* to *or* for *is omitted. Listen to the sentences and change them so the indirect object occurs before the direct object.*

                        direct   indirect
Example: Mother made sandwiches for everyone.
           Mother made everyone sandwiches.

1   2   3   4   5   6   7   8

E. **Listening Comprehension.** *Listen to the passage and try to think of the solution to the question asked at the end of the passage. (See the tape script, page 109.) The answer is found in appendix 5 of* Intensive English for Communication: Book 2. *You will hear the passage and the question twice.*

F. **Dictation.** *Listen and write the sentences. Each sentence will be read three times. Listen to the sentence the first time. Then write the sentence after the second time. Check your written sentence after the third time.*

1. _____

2. _____

3. _____

4. _____

Lesson 6

Making Comparisons

(Listen to the exercises that you hear on the tape as you follow along in your workbook. Try to do all the exercises at least once before looking at the tape script for lesson 6, which is found on page 110.)

Vocabulary Focus[1]

> Verbs of Sight: *See, Look At, Watch, Stare,* and *Observe*
> Look at the definition of each word in your workbook. Then listen to the sentences containing these verbs of sight and repeat them after the speaker.
>
> 1. *See*—know something through the sense of sight
>
>   a. b. c. d.
>
> 2. *Look at*—turn your visual attention to something, either for a brief time or a long time. *Look at* is a more precise and specific than *see*.
>
>   a. b. c. d.
>
> 3. *Watch*—look at something carefully or continuously
>
>   a. b. c. d.
>
> 4. *Stare*—look at something or someone steadily without taking your eyes off that object or person. *Stare* often indicates curiosity.
>
>   a. b. c.
>
> 5. *Observe*—watch attentively as if to make a study of something
>
>   a. b. c. d.

Let's Practice I—Comparison of Adjectives and Adverbs: Comparative and Superlative Degrees

A. Adjectives and Adverbs That Take the Suffix —*er* in the Comparative Degree. *Listen to the sentences and make the comparison that is asked for.*

> *Example:*   A train is fast. What about an airplane?
> **An airplane is faster than a train.**
>
> 1 2 3 4 5 6 7 8 9 10

---

1. This lesson begins with the Vocabulary Focus. The Conversation in *Intensive English for Communication: Book 2*, page 92, is based on a visual chart which cannot be easily adapted to audio recording.

Lesson 6

B. **Adjectives and Adverbs That Form Their Comparative Degree with** *more* **and the Suffix** *—ly*.
Listen to the sentences and make the comparison that is asked for.

Example: A sweater is expensive. What about a coat?
A coat is more expensive than a sweater.

1 2 3 4 5 6 7 8 9 10

C. **Superlative Forms.** *Listen and repeat the sentences after the speaker.*

1 2 3 4 5 6 7 8 9 10

D. **Questions and Answers.** *Listen to the sentences comparing three people or things. Answer the question that follows in the pause provided. You will hear the sentences and questions twice.*

Example: Tom drove 18 kilometers. Frank drove 25 kilometers. Peter went only 10 kilometers. Who drove the farthest of all?
Frank drove the farthest of all.

1 2 3 4 5 6

Let's Practice II—Expressions of Equality, Similarity, and Difference: *As, The Same As, Like,* and *Different From*

A. *Listen to the sentences describing two people or things. Next listen to the comparison using* as *and repeat the comparison after the speaker.*

1 2 3 4 5 6 7 8

B. *Answer these questions using* like, the same as, *or* not the same as *and* different from. *Listen to the examples.*

Examples: Is shampoo like soap?
Yes, shampoo is like soap.
Does the verb *enter* mean the same as *go in*?
Yes, *enter* means the same as *go in*.
Is Japanese the same as Chinese?
No, Japanese is not the same as Chinese. Japanese is different from Chinese.

1 2 3 4 5 6 7 8

Lesson 6

C. **Summary Practice.** *Look at the map of downtown and answer these questions. Pretend that you are the person standing at the X. Answer the questions.*

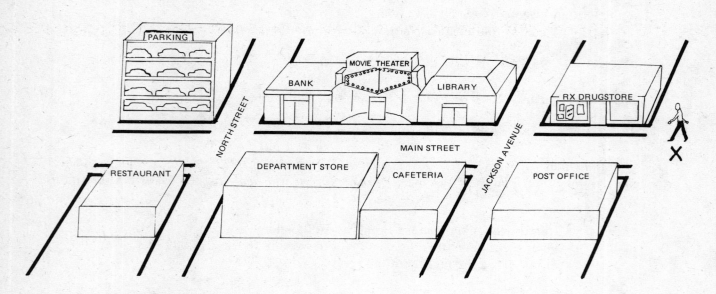

1 2 3 4 5 6 7 8 9 10

Let's Practice III—Expressions of Quantity (Part 1): Count and Noncount Nouns

A. *Make a complete sentence with the expression* **I have** *and the nouns that are given. If the noun is a singular count noun, use the indefinite article* **a**. *If the noun is a noncount noun or a plural count noun, use no article.*

Examples: box
            I have a box.
            boxes
            I have boxes.
            water
            I have water.

1 2 3 4 5 6 7 8 9 10

B. *Repeat the exercise, but this time use* **some** *in front of a noncount noun or a plural count noun. Use* **a** *in front of a singular count noun.*

Examples: box
            I have a box.
            boxes
            I have some boxes.
            water
            I have some water.

1 2 3 4 5 6 7 8 9 10

Lesson 6

C. *This time make a negative sentence using* I don't have. *Use the indefinite article* a *in front of singular count nouns and* any *in front of noncount nouns and plural count nouns.*

Examples: box
I don't have a box.
boxes
I don't have any boxes.
water
I don't have any water.

1 2 3 4 5 6 7 8 9 10

D. **Going Shopping.** *Pretend that you are going shopping for your friends. Ask them if they need certain things. Then answer either* yes *or* no *according to the cue given and use the appropriate expression of quantity,* one, some, *or* any *to replace the noun.*

Examples: soap
Do you need any soap?
Yes. Yes, I need some.
shampoo
Do you need any shampoo?
No. No, I don't need any.
a pen
Do you need a pen?
Yes. Yes, I need one.

1 2 3 4 5 6 7 8

Let's Practice IV—Expressions of Quantity (Part 2): *A Lot Of, A Little, A Few, Enough, Many, and Much*

A. *Listen to the sentences containing an expression of quantity as you read along in your workbook. Write the expression of quantity that you hear in the blank space.*

Example: There's a little water in the glass. _____

Write a little *in the blank space in your workbook.*

1. _____ 6. _____

2. _____ 7. _____

3. _____ 8. _____

4. _____ 9. _____

5. _____ 10. _____

31

Lesson 6

B. ***Too Much* and *Too Many*.** *Listen to the sentence and add a new one with* too much *or* too many.

Example: John used a lot of paint. In fact . . .
In fact, he used too much paint.

1 2 3 4 5 6

C. **True/False.** *Listen to the sentences and the response for each one. If the response is correct, circle* T *in your workbook. If the response is wrong, circle* F *in your workbook.*

Example: Linda Nelson is a medical student at the university. She is very busy and doesn't have much free time these days.
True or false: a. Linda doesn't have too much work to do.   T   F

The answer is false. Circle F *in your workbook.*

b. Linda wants to be a doctor when she finishes her degree.   T   F

The answer is true. Circle T *in your workbook.*

1. a. T F   2. a. T F   3. a. T F

    b. T F   b. T F   b. T F

D. **Dictation.** *Listen and write the sentences. Each sentence will be read three times. Listen to the sentence the first time. Then write the sentence after the second time. Check your written sentence after the third time.*

1. _____

2. _____

 _____

3. _____

 _____

Lesson 7

Houses and Apartments

(Listen to the exercises that you hear on the tape as you follow along in your workbook. Try to do all the exercises at least once before looking at the tape script for lesson 7, which is found on page 116.)

Conversation

At the Housing Office. *Listen to the conversation.*

Receptionist:
Embolo:

Now repeat the sentences after the speaker.

Receptionist:
Embolo:

Vocabulary Focus

Rooms of the House and Furniture

A. *Look at the drawing of the interior of the house and repeat the names of the rooms after the speaker.*

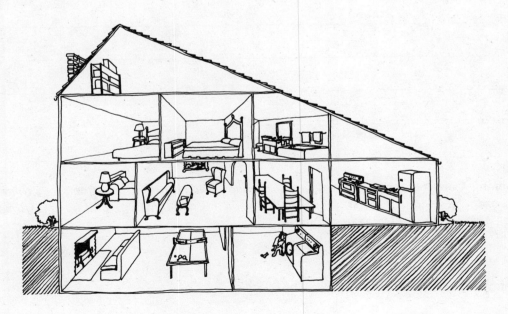

1 2 3 4 5 6 7 8 9 10 11

B. *What furniture is in each room? Look at the drawing as you answer the questions.*

1 2 3 4 5

33

Lesson 7

Let's Practice I—Expressions of Place: *In, At, On*

A. *Look at the drawing of the exterior of Mr. and Mrs. Smith's home. Answer the questions.*

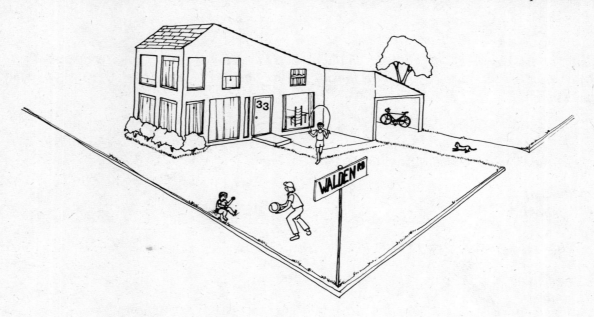

1 2 3 4 5 6 7 8

B. **Listening-Writing Response.** *Listen to the questions and then write the answer in your workbook.*

1. _____
2. _____
3. _____
4. _____
5. _____
6. _____

C. **Listening Comprehension.** *Listen to the passage and the eight questions that follow. Do not answer the questions the first time. You will hear the same passage and the questions a second time. Answer the questions in the pause provided.*

1 2 3 4 5 6 7 8

Let's Practice II—The Definite Article: *The*

A. *A versus **The.** Listen to the sentences as you read along in your workbook. Write the article that you hear, either* a *or* the *on the lines. Remember that* a *changes to* an *before a vowel sound.*

Example: I see _____ house. _____ house is large.

Lesson 7

Write a *in the first blank space and write* the *in the second space.*

1. I bought _____ can of paint. _____ paint was blue.

2. _____ used car that I bought was _____ good deal.

3. _____ little girl found _____ quarter in _____ street.

4. Mother made _____ cake. _____ cake was chocolate.

5. We need _____ extra chair. _____ chair in your room will be fine.

6. Richard caught _____ big fish. _____ fish weighed five kilograms.

7. _____ key is missing. We'll have to have _____ duplicate made.

8. We saw _____ good movie last night. _____ movie won _____ award.

B. **The** versus **No Article.** *Listen to the sentences as you read along in your workbook. Write the article* the *on the line whenever you hear it. If you do not hear* the, *then no article is required. Write an X on the line when no article is used.*

Examples: _____ Captain Harkness flies for Pan American Airlines.

No article is required in this sentence. Put an X in the blank space.

_____ old man is crossing _____ street.

The definite article the *is required in two places. Write* the *in both blank spaces.*

1. _____ Alarm clocks are necessary.

2. _____ alarm clock rang at 6:30 A.M.

3. Have you ever traveled to _____ South America?

4. _____ Queen Elizabeth II travels frequently to _____ other countries.

5. _____ queen is usually accompanied by her husband.

6. _____ telephone was invented by _____ Alexander Graham Bell.

7. We went to _____ Central Park last week.

8. _____ Children were playing in _____ park.

9. Where is _____ Lake Geneva located?

10. _____ Andes are _____ highest mountains in South America.

11. _____ convict was sent to _____ prison.

12. Yesterday I went to _____ class and then to _____ library.

35

Lesson 7

C. Questions about Geography. *Answer the following questions by using a complete sentence.*

Example: What is the longest river in the world? the Nile
The Nile is the longest river in the world.

1 2 3 4

Let's Practice III—Comparison of Nouns: Comparative and Superlative Degrees

A. *Listen to the sentences and answer the question with a complete sentence.*

Example: Ron ate three apples. Liz ate four apples. Who ate more apples?
Liz ate more apples than Ron.

1 2 3 4 5

B. Expression of Equality of Nouns: *As Many As* **and** *As Much As.* *Listen to the sentences and make comparisons according to the example.*

Examples: Paul sees two airplanes and Julie does too.
Julie sees as many airplanes as Paul.
I spent twelve dollars, and you did too.
You spent as much money as I.

1 2 3 4 5 6

Let's Practice IV—Demonstrative Adjectives and Pronouns: *This, These, That,* and *Those*

A. *Listen to the sentences as you read along in your workbook. Write the demonstrative adjective or pronoun that you hear:* this, that, these, *or* those *in the blank spaces.*

Example: _____ chair is red; _____ chair is yellow.

Write this *in the first blank space and* that *in the second space.*

1. _____ book is expensive; _____ one is cheap.

2. _____ pencils are red; _____ pencils are blue.

3. _____ shoes fit me; _____ others don't.

4. _____ glass is larger than _____ one.

5. _____'s not right. _____ is the right answer.

6. _____ students are from China; _____ students are from Japan.

Lesson 7

B. *Another.* Listen to the sentences and add another statement with want *and the pronoun* another one.

Example: I read a good book.
I want to read another one.

1 2 3 4

C. *Other* and *Others.* Listen to the sentences with some *and* other *or* others. *Repeat them after the speaker.*

1 2 3 4 5 6

D. *The Other* and *The Others.* Listen to the conversations and then answer the questions with the cue words that are given for you. Follow the examples.

Examples: We saw two apartments yesterday.
What were they like? big / small
One was big, and the other was small.
We saw three apartments last week.
What were they like? big / small
One was big and the others were small.

1 2 3 4 5

E. **Reading Advertisements.** *Look at the advertisements for apartments in your workbook. As you listen to the speaker, read them aloud.*

1. For rent: two bdr. frn. apt. in mod. build. on quiet st. Utl. pd. $350. Call manager at 922-8671, Mon.-Fri. 5–8 P.M.

2. Available for fall occup.: efficiency apts. on campus. Unfrn. Utl. incl. exc. elect. Large rm w/balc. $190. Call 416-4473

3. Sec. floor: 4 rms. Stove, refrig. & drapes frn. $400 mon. plus elect. First & last mon. rent due upon occup. No pets, no child. Call 382-2569.

4. Green Meadows Apts. Now renting 1 & 2 bdrm. apts. Washer, dryer, dishw. in each apt. Carpet., drapes, rec. facilities. Renting fr. $285. 4141 Green Meadows Blvd. Bellevue. Ph. 597-0839.

F. **Dictation.** *Listen and write the sentences after the speaker.*

1. _____

2. _____

3. _____

_____

Lesson 8

Making Requests and Complaints

(Listen to the exercises that you hear on the tape as you follow along in your workbook. Try to do all the exercises at least once before looking at the tape script for lesson 8, which is found on page 121.)

Conversation

A. **In the Department Store.** *Listen to the conversation between the clerk and the customer.*

   Clerk:
   Customer:

B. **In the Apartment.** *Listen to the conversation between the tenant and the landlord.*

   Tenant:
   Landlord:

C. **At the Complaint Department.** *Listen to the conversation between the customer and the clerk.*

   Customer:
   Clerk:

D. **In the Dormitory.** *Listen to the conversation between the foreign student and the American student. Then answer questions about the dialogue.*

   Foreign student:
   American student:

   1   2   3   4

Vocabulary Focus

1. The Verb *Get*
   Listen to these expressions and sentences which take *get* with the meaning of *become*. Repeat them after the speaker.

   1 2 3 4 5 6 7 8 9 10 11 12 13 14 15 16 17 18 19 20

2. *Be Used To, Get Used To*
   Listen to these sentences and repeat them after the speaker.

   1 2 3 4

Lesson 8

Let's Practice I—Requests and Suggestions

A. **Polite Requests.** *Change these command forms to polite requests by using* will.

   Example: Please help me.
   Will you please help me?

   1 2 3 4 5 6

B. *Repeat the same exercise, only this time use* could *instead of* will *to make a polite request.*

   Example: Please help me.
   Could you please help me?

   1 2 3 4 5

C. **Would You Please?** *What do you say in these situations? Listen and make a polite request with* would you please *by using the verbs given for you. Listen to the example.*

   Example: Someone is knocking at the door. You open the door and see your friend. come in
   Would you please come in?

   1 2 3 4 5

D. **Listening-Writing Response.** *Listen to the conversations using polite request forms and typical responses. In your workbook the first line is given for you. Write in the response that you hear on the tape.*

   Example: Won't you have some coffee?
   Yes, I'd love some.

   Write Yes, I'd love some *in the blank space in your book.*

   1. Won't you have a piece of cake?

      _____

   2. Would you like another cup of coffee?

      _____

   3. Would you please open the window?

      _____

39

Lesson 8

    4. Will you please take a message?

       _____

    5. Could you please mail this letter for me?

       _____

    6. Can you give me a ride home today?

       _____

E. Suggestions with *Let's* and *How About*. *Listen to the suggestion with* let's. *Give the same suggestion using* how about. *Be sure to use the present participle of the verb with* how about.

    Example: Let's finish early today.
               How about finishing early today?

    1 2 3 4 5 6

F. Listening-Writing Response. *Listen to the polite requests and suggestions with* shall *and typical responses. In your workbook part of the dialogue is given for you. Write in the response that you hear on the tape.*

    Example: Shall I open the window?

         *Yes, please do*_____. It's hot in here.

    1. _____. That will be fine.

    2. _____. That will be fun.

    3. _____. The weather isn't good enough.

    4. No, _____!

    5. Sure, _____.

    6. No, _____.

Let's Practice II—Adverbs of Intensification: *Very, Too, Much,* and *Enough*

A. *Listen to the sentences with* very *and add a sentence with* too *according to the example.*

    Example: The student spoke very quietly. The teacher couldn't hear him.
               The student spoke too quietly.

    1 2 3 4 5 6

B. *Answer these questions using* enough *by giving a complete sentence.*

Example: Are you tall enough to touch the ceiling? no
No, I'm not tall enough to touch the ceiling.

1 2 3 4 5

C. Listening Comprehension: A Bad House. *Listen to the passage about a bad house and the five questions that follow. Do not answer the questions the first time. You will hear the same passage and questions again. Answer the questions after the second time.*

1 2 3 4 5

D. A Bad House Continued

1 2 3 4 5

Let's Practice III—Indefinite Expressions: *Someone, No One, Anyone*

A. Listening-Writing Response. *Listen to the dialogues. In your workbook part of the dialogue is given for you. Write in the response that you hear on the tape.*

Example: Is someone at the door?

No, _____ is there.

Write the words no one *in the blank space.*

1. No, _____ is wrong.

2. No, there's _____ who knows the answer.

3. Yes, there's _____ good on TV tonight.

4. Yes, I know _____ about English.

5. I don't like _____ else.

6. No, _____ can help you.

B. *Make new sentences with* no one, nobody, nothing, *or* nowhere *according to the example.*

Example: I didn't ask anyone for help.
I asked no one for help.

1 2 3 4 5 6

Lesson 8

Let's Practice IV—Elliptical Verb Forms

A. **Making Agreements in Affirmative Sentences with the Auxiliary Verb and *Too*.** *Listen to the short dialogue. You will then hear the first line of the dialogue again and a pause for you to add the response.*

Examples: I can speak English.
I can too.
I can speak English.
I can too.

1 2 3 4 5 6

B. **Making Agreements in Affirmative Sentences with *So* and the Auxiliary Verb.** *Listen to the same dialogues that you heard in exercise A. Give a response with* so *according to the example.*

Example: I can speak English.
So can I.
I can speak English.
So can I.

1 2 3 4 5 6

C. **Dictation.** *Listen and write the sentences after the speaker.*

1. _____
2. _____
3. _____
4. _____

Lesson 9

Necessity and Obligation

(Listen to the exercises that you hear on the tape as you follow along in your workbook. Try to do all the exercises at least once before looking at the tape script for lesson 9, which is found on page 127.)

Conversation

Appointment Calendar. Look at Mark Hardin's appointment calendar for the week of February 11. Answer the questions that you hear on the tape.

FEBRUARY	
Sun. 11	Visit Grandfather in hospital. Visiting hours 2-4. Study for chemistry test at night.
Mon. 12	Mail Valentine to Mary Ann. Drop off suit at dry cleaner's. Go to basketball practice - 4:00.
Tues. 13	Dentist appointment - 11:00. Pay parking ticket - $3.00. Basketball game - 8 p.m.
Wed. 14	Valentine's Day. Buy candy for Mary Ann. Send flowers to Mother!
Thurs. 15	Basketball practice - 4:00. Register for photography class at Community College - 7 p.m.
Fri. 16	Pick up suit at cleaner's - a.m. Sign up for Dance Contest - 4:00. Basketball game - 8:00.
Sat. 17	Go to library - a.m. to work on term paper. Dance Contest - School Gym at 9 p.m.

1 2 3 4 5 6 7 8

Vocabulary Focus

The Verb *Take*
Listen to these ten expressions with the verb take. *They come from the list on page 161 of* Intensive English for Communication: Book 2. *Repeat them after the speaker.*

1 2 3 4 5 6 7 8 9 10

Lesson 9

Let's Practice I—Expressions of Necessity: *Must, Have To, Be Required To*

A. *Listen to the sentences with* have to. *Restate the sentences using* must.

Example: I have to stop at a gas station.
I must stop at a gas station.

1 2 3 4

B. *Listen to the sentences with* must *and then put them into the past tense. Remember to use* had to *as the past tense of* must. *Use an appropriate time expression in the past tense.*

Example: They must wash their car this week.
They had to wash their car last week.

1 2 3 4

C. *Listen to the statements and questions with* must *and* have to. *Repeat the same statement or question using the correct form of* be required to.

Examples: Do we have to finish the entire book?
Are we required to finish the entire book?
They had to finish the book.
They were required to finish the book.

1 2 3 4

D. *Complete the phrases that you hear by using* You mustn't *in every case.*

Example: drive fast on a sharp curve
You mustn't drive fast on a sharp curve.

1 2 3 4

E. Making Inferences. *Listen to the situations. Then make an inference using* must *and the cue word or words that are given.*

Example: The little girl is yawning and closing her eyes. sleepy
She must be sleepy.

1 2 3 4 5 6

Let's Practice II—Expressions of Obligation: *Should, Ought To, Had Better,* and *Be Supposed To*

A. *Listen to the sentences with* should. *Restate the sentences with* ought to.

Example: The students should study for the test.
The students ought to study for the test.

1 2 3 4

Lesson 9

B. **What should we do to stay healthy?** *Answer the questions in a complete sentence using either* should *or* shouldn't.

   Examples: Should we eat a good breakfast every morning?
   Yes, we should eat a good breakfast every morning.
   Should we eat only one meal a day?
   No, we shouldn't eat only one meal a day.

   1   2   3   4

C. **Expectations.** *Listen to the situations. Then make statements with* should *meaning* expectation.

   Example: Mary left home an hour ago. I expect that she is at school by now.
   She should be at school by now.

   1   2   3   4   5   6

D. **Listening-Writing Response:** *Should* **versus** *Must*. *Listen to the sentences as you read along in your workbook. Write in the missing words that you hear on the tape.*

   Example: The dentist said I _____ _____ my teeth after every meal.

   Write should *in the first blank space and* brush *in the second.*

   1. You _____ _____ nutritious food at every meal.

   2. You _____ _____ too much sugar during the day.

   3. All living things _____ _____ food and water.

   4. You _____ _____ smoke near gasoline.

   5. People _____ _____ obtain a passport to travel to most foreign countries.

   6. They _____ _____ until the last minute to apply for their passport.

Let's Practice III—Past of Modal Auxiliary Verbs (Part 1): *Must Have* **and** *Should Have*

A. *Listen to the sentences as you read along in your workbook. Make an inference about each one in the past tense using* must have *and the verb expression given for you. Follow the example.*

   Examples: They are still shaking. be frightened
   They must have been frightened.
   A policeman stopped the man on the freeway. be speeding
   He must have been speeding.

   1   2   3   4   5   6

Lesson 9

B. *Listen to the sentences as you read along in your workbook. Make a statement about each one in the past tense using* should have *and the verb given for you.*

Example: I didn't pass the test. study harder
I should have studied harder.

1. They were late. be on time
2. The student was sleeping in class. listening to the teacher
3. Their plane is supposed to arrive at noon. It's almost noon. be arriving now
4. I took a very boring course. not take it
5. The bus usually gets here at nine. It's twenty after nine now and the bus still isn't here. come by now
6. The students got into trouble with their math teacher. not be passing notes

C. Listening-Writing Response. *Make inferences about the past. Listen to the situation and then write a logical answer using* must have.

Example: The dog got out of the yard.

Now ask yourself what must have happened. For instance, someone must have left the gate open *or* the dog must have jumped over the fence. *Either answer is correct. Write one of these answers in the blank space in your workbook or write another answer that is also possible. Listen to the situation again:*

The dog got out of the yard.

_____

1. _____

2. _____

3. _____

4. _____

D. Listening-Writing Response. *Use* should have *or* shouldn't have *in response to the situations that you hear. Write your answers in your workbook just as you did in exercise C.*

Example: Jerry was watching TV at three in the morning.
What should he have been doing instead?

Now write He should have been sleeping *or* He should have been in bed, *or any other logical response to the question.*

_____

1. _____

2. _____

Lesson 9

3. _____

4. _____

E. **Listening Comprehension.** *Listen to the story about Eddie Cox and then answer the questions. You will hear the story and questions two times. Wait until the second time to answer the questions.*

1 2 3 4 5 6 7

Let's Practice IV—*Both* and *Each, Either . . . Or,* and *Neither . . . Nor*

A. **Listening-Reading Response: True/False.** *Listen to the sentences. In your workbook read the two responses for each sentence. If the response is correct, circle T in the answer column. If the answer is not correct, circle F. You will hear each sentence twice.*

Example: Tom wants a dog for a pet or else he wants a cat.

Now read to yourself sentences a *and* b *in your workbook and decide if they are true or false.*

a. Tom wants both a dog and a cat for a pet.	T F
b. Tom wants either a dog or a cat for a pet.	T F

Sentence a *is false. Circle* F *in the answer column.*
Sentence b *is true. Circle* T *in the answer column.*

1. a. Mr. Smith went to look for a new car and so did Mrs. Smith.   T F

   b. Mr. Smith went without Mrs. Smith to look for a new car.   T F

2. a. Mr. Smith likes a couple of the cars in the display room.   T F

   b. Mr. Smith likes the two cars in the display room.   T F

3. a. One car is just as good as the other car.   T F

   b. One car has better features than the other car.   T F

4. a. George neither smokes cigarettes nor drinks alcohol.   T F

   b. George either smokes cigarettes or drinks alcohol.   T F

5. a. Mary and Tom will both help you.   T F

   b. Mary can help you but Tom probably can't.   T F

6. a. Only one of the students knows the answer.   T F

   b. Both of the students don't know the answer.   T F

Lesson 9

B. Dictation. *Listen and write the sentences after the speaker.*

1. _____
   _____
2. _____
3. _____
4. _____

Lesson 10
Can You Drive a Car?

Conversation

How to Drive Safely. *Listen to the instructions for operating an automobile and some advice for driving safely.*

1 2 3 4 5 6 7 8 9 10

Now repeat the instructions after the speaker.

Vocabulary Focus

Parts of the Car
Look at the picture of the sports car and find the parts that you hear on the tape. Repeat the parts of the car after the speaker.

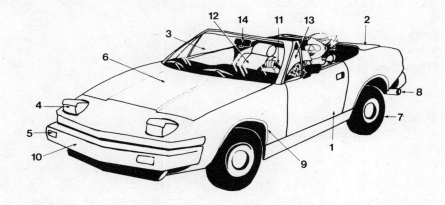

Exterior: 1 2 3 4 5 6 7 8 9 10
Interior: 11 12 13 14

Let's Practice I—Expressions of Ability: *Can, Could,* and *Be Able*

A. *Listen to both affirmative and negative sentences with* can *and* could. *Then say the same sentence using* be able.

Examples: I can speak English.
I'm able to speak English.
I couldn't finish all the work.
I wasn't able to finish all the work.

1 2 3 4 5 6 7 8 9 10

Lesson 10

B. Listening-Writing Response. *Write answers to the questions in complete sentences.*

Example: Are you able to play tennis?

Yes, I'm able to play tennis.

or: *No, I'm not able to play tennis.*

1. _____
2. _____
3. _____
4. _____
5. _____
6. _____

C. Listening Comprehension. *Listen to the short dialogue and the question. You will hear them a second time. Answer the question after the second time.*

Example: John couldn't go to the party last night.
Why not?
His wife and children were sick.
Oh, that's too bad.

Question: Why wasn't John able to go to the party last night?
Because his wife and children were sick.

1 2 3

Let's Practice II—Expressions of Permission: *May, Can, Allow, Let,* and *Be Allowed To*

A. *Ask permission using* may *and the expression given for you.*

Example: I / borrow two dollars from you
May I borrow two dollars from you?

1 2 3 4 5 6

B. Listening-Writing Response. *Listen to the short dialogue as you read along in your workbook. Then repeat the dialogue after the speaker and write the words that are missing in the blank space in your workbook.*

Lesson 10

Example: Can we smoke in the classroom?
No, you're not allowed to.
Can we smoke in the classroom?

No, you're ___not allowed to___.

1. No, you're _____.

2. No, you can't. The management _____.

3. Yes, certainly, _____.

4. No, you're _____.

5. No, the landlord _____ them.

6. No, you _____.

C. Listening-Writing Response. *Write answers to the questions in the blank spaces in your workbook. Each question will be heard twice.*

1. _____
2. _____
3. _____
4. _____

D. True or False? *Listen to the first statement concerning medical care. Then listen to the second statement and tell if it correctly summarizes the first statement. If the second statement is correct, circle* T. *If the statement is incorrect, circle* F.

Example: The doctor said to the patient, "You will have to undergo surgery."
The patient was required to undergo surgery.   T F

The second statement summarizes the first one. Therefore it is true. Circle T *in your workbook.*

1. T F   4. T F

2. T F   5. T F

3. T F   6. T F

Lesson 10

E. Road Signs. *Look at the pictures of the road signs in your workbook as you listen to the meaning of the signs. Locate and point to the appropriate picture as you hear the sign and repeat it after the speaker. There are twenty road signs all together.*

1 2 3 4 5 6 7 8 9 10 11 12 13 14 15 16 17 18 19 20

Let's Practice III—Making Questions by Rising Intonation

A. Surprise Questions. *Listen to the surprise questions and short answers. You will hear them twice. After the second time repeat the questions and answers after the speaker.*

Example: John was sick yesterday?
  Yes, he was.
  John was sick yesterday?
  Yes, he was.

1 2 3 4

B. *Change the statements to surprise questions by using rising intonation.*

Example: Ted's brother was fired yesterday.
  Ted's brother was fired yesterday?

1 2 3 4 5 6

C. *Listen to the statements and respond with a short surprise question using rising intonation.*

Example: Doug left because he found a better job.
  He did?

1 2 3 4 5 6

Let's Practice IV—Tag Questions

A. *Listen to the rising intonation pattern that occurs in affirmative tag questions to indicate uncertainty. Do not repeat the sentences out loud at this time.*

52

Lesson 10

1 2 3 4 5

Now repeat the sentences after the speaker.

B. *Listen to the falling intonation pattern that occurs in affirmative tag questions to indicate certainty and that the speaker expects agreement from the listener. Do not repeat the sentences out loud at this time.*

1 2 3 4 5

Now repeat the sentences after the speaker.

C. **Negative Tags.** *Listen to the rising intonation pattern that occurs in negative tag questions to indicate uncertainty. Do not repeat the sentences out loud at this time.*

1 2 3 4 5

Now repeat the sentences after the speaker.

D. *Listen to the falling intonation pattern that occurs in negative tag questions to indicate certainty and that the speaker expects agreement from the listener. Do not repeat the sentences out loud at this time.*

1 2 3 4 5

Now repeat the sentences after the speaker.

E. **Pronunciation of Tags in Rapid Speech.** *Listen to these sentences in normal, rapid speech and hear how the pronunciation of tags with* you *and* he *is altered. Do not repeat these sentences; listen only.*

1 2 3 4 5 6 7 8 9 10 11 12 13 14

F. *Listen to the sentences, repeat them, and add the appropriate tag. In the first four sentences, use a rising intonation and in the last four, use a falling intonation.*

Example: You went there yesterday.
You went there yesterday, didn't you?

1 2 3 4 5 6 7 8

G. **Dictation.** *Listen and write the sentences after the speaker.*

1. _____

2. _____

3. _____

4. _____

Lesson 11
Looking for a Job

Conversation

A. **Help Wanted.** *Listen to the conversation.*

Alex:
Mike:

Now repeat the conversation after the speaker.

Alex:
Mike:

B. **I Need a Job.** *Listen to the conversation.*

Student:
Counselor:

Now repeat the conversation after the speaker.

Student:
Counselor:

C. **I Can Sell Anything.** *Listen to the conversation.*

Mr. Kirby:
Fred:

D. **You're fired!** *Listen to the conversation.*

Manager:
Clayton:

Now repeat the conversation after the speaker.

Vocabulary Focus

Occupations
Listen to the words that fall into the category of occupations. Repeat them after the speaker.

Nouns: 1 2 3 4 5 6
Verbs: 7 8 9 10 11 12 13

Lesson 11

Let's Practice I—Expressions of Possibility: *May, Might, Can, Could,* and *It's Possible That*

A. *Listen to the sentences and change them by using* may.

   Example: Maybe I will clean my room this afternoon.
   I may clean my room this afternoon.

   1 2 3 4

B. *Do the same exercise as A, but this time use* might *instead of* may.

   Example: Maybe I will move soon.
   I might move soon.

   1 2 3 4

C. *Answer these questions of possibility by using a complete sentence. Use the cue words that are given for you.*

   Example: Where can we get a good meal in this town? at the Mayfair restaurant
   You can get a good meal at the Mayfair restaurant.

   1 2 3 4 5 6

D. *Restate each sentence using could instead of the expression* it is possible that.

   Example: It is possible that I will get my degree next year.
   I could get my degree next year.

   1 2 3

E. *Do the same exercise as D, but this time use* might *instead of* could.

   Example: It is possible that I will get my degree next year.
   I might get my degree next year.

   1 2 3

Let's Practice II—Past of Modal Auxiliary Verbs (Part 2): *May Have, Might Have,* and *Could Have*

A. *Listen to the situations. You will hear each situation twice. After the second time repeat the response that is given.*

   Example: I just called Lynn who said she never received my invitation.
   You may have forgotten to mail it.
   I just called Lynn who said she never received my invitation.
   You may have forgotten to mail it.

   1 2 3 4 5 6

55

Lesson 11

B. **Listening-Writing Response.** *Listen to some more situations. You will hear each situation twice. After the second time repeat the response that is given and write it in your workbook.*

Example: Jimmy's glasses are broken and his nose is bleeding.
What could have happened?
He could have been in a fight.
Jimmy's glasses are broken and his nose is bleeding.
What could have happened?

He could have been in a fight.

1. _____, but the other team surprised us.

2. _____ back to California.

3. _____ the test.

4. Mr. Morris _____ an accident on the road.

C. **Listening Comprehension.** *Listen to each sentence and to the two responses that are given. Choose the appropriate response that best describes the sentence. Sometimes both responses will be correct. Circle* a *or* b *in your workbook, whichever you think is the correct choice.*

Examples: I could have taken the train, but it left too late.
   a. You took the train.
   b. You didn't take the train.

Answer b *is correct. Circle* b *in your workbook.*

Bob could have gone to London last week.
   a. It's possible that Bob went to London last week.
   b. We aren't certain if Bob went to London.

Both answers are correct. Circle a *and* b *in your workbook.*

1. a. b.   5. a. b.

2. a. b.   6. a. b.

3. a. b.   7. a. b.

4. a. b.   8. a. b.

Lesson 11

Let's Practice III—Past Perfect Tense and Future Perfect Tense

A. *Change the sentences from the present perfect to the past perfect tense.*

Examples: Jack has sent the letter, hasn't he?
Jack had sent the letter, hadn't he?
He hasn't forgotten it, has he?
He hadn't forgotten it, had he?

1 2 3 4 5

B. *Listen to the dialogues. You will hear each dialogue twice. Repeat the entire dialogue after the speaker the second time.*

Example: Where are you living now?
I'm living in Lakeland.
How long had you lived in your country before you came to Lakeland?
I had lived in my country for twenty years before I came to Lakeland.

1 2 3

C. Future Perfect. *Answer the questions in a complete sentence by using the cue words given for you.*

Example: Do you think you will have finished this lesson by the end of the hour. yes
Yes, I think I will have finished this lesson by the end of the hour.

1 2 3 4 5 6

Let's Practice IV—Subordinating Conjunctions: *Before* and *After*

A. *Combine the sentences using* before.

Example: I wash my face. Then I brush my teeth.
I wash my face before I brush my teeth.

1 2 3 4 5 6

B. *Combine the same sentences as in exercise A, only this time using the conjunction* after.

Example: I wash my face. Then I brush my teeth.
I brush my teeth after I wash my face.

1 2 3 4

Lesson 11

C. Listening Comprehension. *Listen to each sentence and to the two responses that are given. Choose the appropriate response that best describes the sentence. Circle* a *or* b *in your workbook, whichever you think is the correct choice.*

Example: John ate his dinner and then he went to the movies.
    a. John ate his dinner before he went to the movies.
    b. John ate his dinner after he went to the movies.

Answer a *is correct. Circle* a *in your workbook.*

1. a. b.   5. a. b.

2. a. b.   6. a. b.

3. a. b.   7. a. b.

4. a. b.   8. a. b.

D. Dictation. *Listen and write the sentences.*

1. _____

2. _____

3. _____

4. _____

Lesson 12

On the Road

Conversation

A. **Making Travel Plans.** *Listen to the conversation.*

Pierre:
Bill:

Now repeat the conversation after the speaker.

Pierre:
Bill:

B. **Returning Home.** *Listen to the conversation.*

Pierre:
Bill:

Now repeat the conversation after the speaker.

Pierre:
Bill:

Vocabulary Focus

Indefinite *You, They,* and *One*
Listen to the sentences where you, they, *and* one *mean* everybody *or* all people. *Repeat them after the speaker.*

1 2 3 4 5 6

2. The Verbs *Make* and *Do*
A. *Listen to certain expressions that are used with* make *and* do. *A complete list can be found on page 227 of* Intensive English for Communication: Book 2.

Make: 1 2 3 4 5 6 7 8 9 10 11 12 13 14 15 16 17 18 19 20
Do: 1 2 3 4 5 6 7 8 9 10 11 12

Lesson 12

B. *Choose the correct word,* make *or* do, *for each sentence. Circle either* make *or* do *in your workbook.*

Example: How many telephone calls do you usually   make   do   every week?

Make *is the correct answer. Circle* make *in your workbook.*

1. made   done
2. make   do
3. making   doing
4. make   do
5. made   do

6. making   doing
7. make   do
8. made   done
9. made   did
10. make   do

Let's Practice I—Conditional Clauses with *If* (Part 1): Present

A. *Listen to the sentences and then combine them by using* if.

Example: I may be sick tomorrow. Then I'll stay home.
If I am sick tomorrow, I'll stay home.

1   2   3   4

B. **What will happen if . . . ?** *Answer the questions in a complete sentence using the cue words given for you.*

Example: What will happen if it rains tomorrow? take my umbrella
If it rains tomorrow, I'll take my umbrella.

1   2   3   4

C. **Listening-Writing Response.** *Listen to the first part of the sentences as you read along in your workbook. Complete the sentences with a logical response. Write in your workbook.*

1. _____
2. _____
3. _____
4. _____

D. **Hypothetical Situations.** *Change the sentences from real conditions to hypothetical conditions. In the first three sentences use* would *or* wouldn't *in the main clause; in sentences four through six, use the contraction, apostrophe* d ('d), *in affirmative sentences.*

Example: If I forget my pen, I'll have to borrow one from somebody.
If I forgot my pen, I would have to borrow one from somebody.

1   2   3   4   5   6

E. *Listen to the dialogues the first time. Then repeat both parts after the speaker the second time.*

Example: What would happen if you forgot your English book?
Oh, I'd borrow my friend's.
What would happen if you forgot your English book?
Oh, I'd borrow my friend's.

1 2 3

F. *Change these conditional sentences by using* could *in the main clause.*

Example: We can come if she invites us.
We could come if she invited us.

1 2 3 4

G. *Listen to the sentences and restate them by using* could *in the* if *clause and* would *or apostrophe* d ('d) *in the main clause.*

Example: I will do the work if I can.
I would do the work if I could.

1 2 3 4

Let's Practice II—Conditional Clauses with *Unless* and Conditional Clauses with *If* (Part 2): Past

A. *Listen to the sentences and change the* if *clause to* unless.

Example: Mary will come tomorrow if she isn't sick.
Mary will come tomorrow unless she's sick.

1 2 3 4

B. *Practice* unless *in hypothetical statements by changing the* if *clauses to* unless *clauses.*

Example: If you had a car, you could drive to San Francisco.
Unless you had a car, you couldn't drive to San Francisco.

1 2 3 4

C. **Conditional Clauses in the Past.** *Change the hypothetical statements to the past.*

Example: If I had a lot of money now, I would travel around the world.
If I had had a lot of money last year, I would have traveled around the world.

1 2 3 4

Lesson 12

D. *Answer these questions in a complete sentence by using the cue words that are given.*

Example: Would Frank have borrowed money if he hadn't needed it? no
No, Frank wouldn't have borrowed money if he hadn't needed it.

1   2   3   4

E. Listening-Reading Response. *Listen to the sentences. In your workbook read the two responses for each sentence and circle the one that is appropriate.*

Example: What would you have been doing today if you hadn't come to class?
    a. I would have stayed home or else gone shopping.
    b. I would have come to class.

The appropriate answer is a. *Circle* a *in your workbook.*

1. a.   b.   3. a.   b.

2. a.   b.   4. a.   b.

Let's Practice III—Reported Speech and Indirect Questions

A. *Listen to the sentences and then change the direct speech to reported speech.*

Example: Henry says, "I have to pass the course."
Henry says he has to pass the course.

1   2   3   4

B. *Repeat the exercise, but this time the verbs will be in the past tense.*

Example: Henry said, "I have to pass the course."
Henry said he had to pass the course.

1   2   3   4

C. *Listen to the sentences and put them into the past tense.*

Example: Mark thinks we're arriving today.
Mark thought we were arriving today.

1   2   3   4   5   6   7   8

D. Indirect Questions. *Listen to the questions and the cue question given. Then make an indirect question.*

Example: Which car was blue? Do you remember?
Do you remember which car was blue?

1   2   3   4   5   6

Lesson 12

E. *Answer the questions in a complete sentence. Begin each sentence with* I don't know.

Example: What time is it?
I don't know what time it is.

1 2 3 4

F. **Listening Comprehension.** *Listen to the passage and the questions that follow. Do not answer the questions the first time. You will hear the same passage and the questions a second time. Answer the questions in the pause provided.*

1 2 3 4

Let's Practice IV—Possessive Nouns

A. *Answer the questions by using the possessive form of the noun or name that is given for you.*

Example: Whose pen is this? Mary
It's Mary's pen.

1 2 3 4 5 6

B. *Listen to the sentences and then give the alternate possessive form with* of.

Example: The city's problems are increasing.
The problems of the city are increasing.

1 2 3 4 5 6

C. **Dictation.** *Listen and write the sentences after the speaker.*

1. _____

2. _____

63

Lesson 13

Writing a Letter

Conversation

A. A Letter of Application. *Listen to the conversation.*

Ali:
Ben:

Now repeat the conversation after the speaker.

Ali:
Ben:

B. A While Later. *Listen to the conversation.*

Ben:
Ali:

Now repeat the conversation after the speaker.

Ben:
Ali:

Vocabulary Focus

The Verbs *Say, Tell, Speak,* and *Talk*
Listen to the sentences as you read along in your workbook. Write in the verb that you hear.

1. Can you __*tell*__ me where I can get some information about the National Parks in the United States?

2. Why don't you go to the reference department of the public library and _____ to someone. They will either give you the information or _____ you where to find it.

3. Excuse me. Please _____ me that address again. I didn't hear what you _____ after "Parks."

4. I _____ you can write to Parks, Washington, D.C. 20340. They will _____ you all about the Grand Canyon, Yosemite, Yellowstone Park, the Smoky Mountains, and many other places.

Lesson 13

5. I _____ to my biology professor yesterday for a few minutes. He is a well-known scientist who recently _____ at an international conference on pollution and the environment. During our conversation, he _____ that he was going on a canoe trip to Michigan this summer.

Let's Practice I—Verbals: Infinitives

A. *Listen to the sentence and then make a new sentence by using the infinitive as subject.*

   Example: It's easy for a cat to climb a tree.
   To climb a tree is easy for a cat.

   1 2 3 4 5 6

B. *Answer the questions by using the cue words that are given for you.*

   Example: What is important for you to do? study English
   It's important for me to study English.

   1 2 3 4

C. **Listening Comprehension.** *Listen to the short conversations and then answer the questions. The conversation and the questions will be heard twice.*

   Example: What sports do you like to do?
   I like to swim and play tennis.
   Would you like to play tennis with me tomorrow?
   Yes, I'd love to.

   Questions: What sports does the girl like to do?
   The girl likes to swim and play tennis.
   What does the boy invite the girl to do with him?
   The boy invites the girl to play tennis with him.

   1 2

D. *Listen to the questions and answer the questions using the cue words given for you.*

   Example: Tom passed his driver's test. What was he qualified to do? drive a car
   He was qualified to drive a car.

   1 2 3 4

Lesson 13

E. **Listening Comprehension: True or False?** *Listen to the sentences and the responses. If the responses are logical or possible, circle* true *in the answer column. If they are not logical or possible, circle* false. *You will hear each sentence and response two times.*

Example: The students studied hard during the course.
They weren't prepared to take the final exam. T F

The answer is false. Circle false *(F) in the answer column.*

The students studied hard during the course.
They were prepared to take the final exam. T F

The answer is true. *Circle* true *(T) in the answer column.*

1. T F
2. T F
3. T F
4. T F
5. T F
6. T F

Let's Practice II—Gerunds

A. *Listen to the sentences with an infinitive subject and make a new sentence beginning with a gerund subject.*

Example: To learn another language takes a long time.
Learning another language takes a long time.

1 2 3 4 5 6

B. **Listening-Writing Response.** *Listen to the sentences as you read along in your workbook. Write in the gerund that you hear.*

Example: We enjoyed ___*taking*___ a walk.

1. When did you finish _____?

2. Do you enjoy _____?

3. Our team kept on _____, so we were pleased.

4. Did they say they were sorry for _____ late?

5. _____ animals is interesting.

6. Would you mind _____ Connie too?

Lesson 13

C. Verbs Which Take Both an Infinitive and a Gerund. *Listen to the sentences and then make a new sentence by giving the alternate construction.*

Examples: We continued to read the paper.
We continued reading the paper.
Ted loves playing football.
Ted loves to play football.

1 2 3 4 5 6

D. *Practice the verbs* stop *and* remember *followed by the infinitive or a gerund. Listen to the situations and answer the questions by using the cue words given for you.*

Examples: We pulled into a restaurant and stopped the car.
What did we stop doing? driving
We stopped driving.
What did we stop to do? eat something
We stopped to eat something.

1 2 3 4 5

Let's Practice III—Verbs That Take a Noun Followed by the Infinitive and Verbs and Adjectives of Desire, Necessity, and Urgency Followed by a Noun Clause

A. *Listen to the dialogues. You will then hear the first line of the dialogue a second time followed by a pause for you to give the first line.*

Example: What did the doctor ask the nurse to do?
The doctor asked the nurse to take the patient's temperature.
What did the doctor ask the nurse to do?
The doctor asked the nurse to take the patient's temperature.

1 2 3 4 5 6

B. Listening, Reading, and Answering Questions. *Listen to the passage as you read along in your workbook. Then answer the questions orally that you hear on the tape.*

Saving Energy

The president of the United States has urged that Americans save energy in a number of ways. First, he has requested that people lower their thermostats to 65 degrees Fahrenheit in the winter. He has suggested that everyone wear extra clothing to keep warm. Second, he has directed that the gasoline tax be raised. He has also proposed that the consumption of gasoline for automobiles be cut down. He has recommended that people form car pools to drive to work. Third, he has advised that everyone use less electricity at home and that people not waste water. Fourth, he has pleaded that the petroleum industry not rely totally on imported oil for its sales, but instead that companies drill for new wells in the United States. Moreover, he has demanded that other sources of energy be investigated, such as solar energy. Finally, he has insisted that Congress pass an energy program which would help solve the nation's energy crisis.

1 2 3 4 5 6

Lesson 13

C. *Answer the questions in a complete sentence with the cue words that are given for you.*

Example: What is necessary that the teacher do over the weekend? prepare for her class
It's necessary that the teacher prepare for her class over the weekend.

1 2 3 4

Let's Practice IV—Verbs Followed by a Noun and a Gerund and Verbs Followed by a Noun with a Preposition and a Gerund

A. *Answer the questions in a complete sentence with the cue words given for you.*

Example: What animal did you hear barking? a dog
I heard a dog barking.

1 2 3 4 5

B. *Answer the questions in a complete sentence with the cue words given for you.*

Example: What did Nancy thank Mrs. Jones for? watching her children
Nancy thanked Mrs. Jones for watching her children.

1 2 3 4

C. **Listening Comprehension.** *Listen to the passage and then answer the questions. You will hear the passage and questions two times. Wait until the second time to answer the questions.*

1 2 3 4 5 6 7

D. **Dictation.** *Listen and write the sentences after the speaker.*

1. _____

2. _____
   _____

3. _____

4. _____

5. _____

Lesson 14

Sports and Recreation

Conversation

Look at the pictures and answer the questions.

1 2 3 4 5 6

Lesson 14

Vocabulary Focus

Sports and Recreational Activities

1. *Listen to the expressions that take* go *plus the present participle of the main verb. Repeat them after the speaker.*

   1 2 3 4 5 6 7 8 9 10 11 12 13 14 15 16 17 18 19 20 21

2. *Listen to the expressions of sports and games that take the verb* play. *Repeat them after the speaker.*

   1 2 3 4 5 6 7 8 9 10 11 12 13 14 15 16 17 18 19 20 21

Let's Practice I—Expressions of Preference: *Would Rather, Prefer,* and *Like Better*

A. *Make up conversations using* would you rather *with the cue words that are given. Complete the conversation by answering* I'd rather *with the cue word that you hear.*

   Example: tennis or golf
   Would you rather play tennis or golf?
   tennis
   I'd rather play tennis.

   1 2 3 4 5

B. *Listen to the conversation. You will then hear the first line of the conversation again with a pause for you to give the correct response.*

   Example: I prefer to drive to work than to take the bus. How about you?
   I prefer to drive to work too.
   I prefer to drive to work than to take the bus. How about you?
   I prefer to drive to work too.

   1 2 3 4

C. **Listening Comprehension.** *Listen to the short conversation and then answer the questions. The conversation and the questions will be heard twice.*

   Example: Which do you like better, tennis or bowling?
   I like tennis better.
   O.K. Let's go play tennis this afternoon.

   Question: Which game does the girl like better?
   She likes tennis better.

   1 2 3

Lesson 14

Let's Practice II—Verbs with Inseparable Particles, Verbs with Separable Particles, and Verbs Plus a Preposition

A. **Verbs with Inseparable Particles.** *Repeat these verbs and the following sentences after the speaker.*

1 2 3 4 5 6 7 8

B. **Verbs with Separable Particles.** *Listen to the sentences and give the alternate form of the verb plus particle.*

Example: Ted put away his clothes.
Ted put his clothes away.

1 2 3 4 5 6

C. **Using Particles with Pronouns.** *Listen to these sentences about "contrary Hank," a boy who never obeys his mother. Whatever she says, he does the opposite. Tell what Hank did or didn't do according to the example.*

Examples: Hank's mother said, "Turn on the light."
But he didn't turn it on.
Hank's mother said, "Don't turn on the TV."
But he turned it on.

1 2 3 4 5 6

D. **Verbs Plus Preposition: Listening-Writing Response.** *Listen to the sentences as you read along in your workbook. Fill in the preposition that you hear in the blank space.*

Example: I looked _____ the report yesterday.
Write the preposition at *in your workbook.*

1. I spoke _____ John briefly when I saw him this morning.

2. Don't sit _____ the floor.

3. We waited _____ the bus in the rain.

4. Did you think _____ me while I was gone?

5. Have you ever heard _____ a bird that couldn't fly?

6. The coach insisted _____ good discipline for his team.

7. Farmers must look _____ their crops and animals.

Lesson 14

  8. What countries in Europe did you drive _____?

  9. The girl asked _____ the actor's autograph.

  10. Mr. Warner had to take care _____ some business before he left town.

E. *Listen to the sentences and make a new sentence by substituting a pronoun for the object noun according to the example.*

   Example: We listened to the radio.
   We listened to it.

   1 2 3 4 5 6

F. **Summary Practice.** *Distinguish between verbs that take a particle and verbs that take a preposition. Listen to the sentences and then make a new sentence by substituting a pronoun for the object noun of the first sentence.*

   Examples: Richard brought out his guitar.
   Richard brought it out.
   We looked for the key.
   We looked for it.

   1 2 3 4 5 6 7 8

Let's Practice III—Expressions of Cause and Effect and Expressions of Contrast

A. *Listen to the sentences and, keeping the same order, connect them by using the conjunction* because. *In some cases* because *will come at the beginning of the sentence and in other cases* because *will come at the end.*

   Examples: Harry was going 80 miles per hour. He got a ticket for speeding.
   Because Harry was going 80 miles per hour, he got a ticket for speeding.
   Judy got a ticket for speeding. She was going 80 miles per hour.
   Judy got a ticket for speeding because she was going 80 miles per hour.

   1 2 3 4 5 6

B. *Because Of. Listen to the sentences and make new ones using* because of.

   Example: We didn't like the restaurant because the service was poor.
   We didn't like the restaurant because of the poor service.

   1 2 3 4 5

C. **Listening-Writing Response.** *Listen to the sentences as you read along in your workbook. Fill in the blank space with the correct word that you hear on the tape.*

   Example: We all went swimming _____ the water was warm.

   Write the word since *in your workbook.*

1. _____ we ran out of bread, we couldn't have toast for breakfast.

2. My parents moved to Arizona _____ it has a dry climate.

3. Ali missed the test _____ he came too late.

4. We looked for another apartment _____ the landlord was going to raise our rent.

5. I like Florida _____ its climate.

6. _____ Mr. Leonard couldn't stand crowds, he avoided big cities.

D. **Listening-Reading Response: True/False.** *Listen to the sentences. In your workbook read the two restatements of each sentence. If the restatement is correct and logical, circle* true *(T) in the answer column. If the restatement is not correct or logical, circle* false *(F). You will hear each sentence twice.*

Example: Oscar went to bed early although he wasn't very tired.

a. Oscar went to bed early because he was very tired. T F

b. Oscar went to bed early, but he wasn't very tired. T F

Sentence a *is false. Circle* F *in the answer column.*
Sentence b *is true. Circle* T *in the answer column.*

1. a. Mountain climbing is a popular sport because of its danger. T F

   b. Mountain climbing is a popular sport in spite of its danger. T F

2. a. We had a good time on the camping trip even though there were many mosquitos. T F

   b. We enjoyed the camping trip, but there were a lot of mosquitos. T F

3. a. Carl visited Sweden although his mother lives there. T F

   b. Since Carl's mother lives in Sweden, he went there for a visit. T F

4. a. Because of reports of a blizzard, we headed north. T F

   b. We headed north although there were reports of a blizzard. T F

Lesson 14

    5. a. Kevin used to go to Silver Lake every summer but he didn't like to fish.   T   F

       b. Kevin used to go to Silver Lake every summer in spite of the good fishing.   T   F

    6. a. Mr. Hawthorne is a happy person in spite of the fact that he doesn't have a lot of money.   T   F

       b. Mr. Hawthorne needs a lot of money to enjoy life.   T   F

E. **Listening, Reading, and Writing Response.** *Listen to the passage as you read along in your workbook. Then you will have a sentence completion exercise to do. You will hear the first half of the sentence on the tape. Then there will be a pause for you to fill in the rest of the sentence in the blank space in your workbook. Remember, you are not writing a complete sentence, only the second half of a sentence. Note that the example is done for you.*

Canoeing

    Canoeing is increasing in popularity in North America because of people's interest in the outdoors. One of the best canoeing areas in the United States stretches from Rainy Lake Minnesota, to Lake Superior. It is part of Superior National Forest. There, over 160,000 people a year paddle down trails that run through streams and lakes for hundreds of miles. They come in bad weather as well as good weather.

    The first canoes were made from trees and bark by the North American Indians, who used them as a means of transportation. In the early days of American history, French fur traders also found canoes a convenience. Now canoes are made out of lightweight materials, such as aluminum. Their purpose is for outdoor sports and recreation.

Now complete the sentences that you hear on the tape.

Example: Canoeing is gaining in popularity because

    _____ *people are interested in the outdoors* _____.

In your workbook you see that the sentence has been completed for you. Read the sentence to yourself.

1. _____

2. _____

3. _____

4. _____

5. _____

Lesson 14

Let's Practice IV—Result Clauses and *Whether Or Not*

A. *Answer the questions by using the cue words given for you.*

Example: What is so high that you can't touch it? the sky
The sky is so high that you can't touch it.

1 2 3 4

B. *Answer the questions using* whether or not.

Example: Will you go to the park if it rains?
I will go to the park whether or not it rains.

1 2 3 4 5 6

C. Dictation. *Write the sentences after the speaker.*

1. _____
   _____

2. _____
   _____

3. _____

Lesson 15
Education and Future Plans

Conversation

A. The End of Summer. *Listen to the conversation.*

Nancy:
Beth:

Now repeat the conversation after the speaker.

Nancy:
Beth:

B. After Graduation from College. *Listen to the conversation.*

Mrs. Baker:
Kathy:
Mrs. Baker:
Jerry:
Mrs. Baker:
Patty:

Now repeat the conversation after the speaker.

Mrs. Baker:
Kathy:
Mrs. Baker:
Jerry:
Mrs. Baker:
Patty:

Vocabulary Focus

Educational Institutions in the United States
Listen to the various schools and educational programs. Repeat them after the speaker. An explanation of each school or program can be found on pages 300 through 302 of Intensive English for Communication: Book 2.

1 2 3 4 5 6 7 8 9 10 11 12 13 14 15 16

Lesson 15

Let's Practice I—Expressions with Verbs and Adjectives That Take Particles and/or Prepositions

A. *Listen and repeat the verbs plus particle plus preposition and the following sentences.*

   Example: drop in on
                I dropped in on John yesterday.
                I dropped in on him.

1 2 3 4 5 6

B. *Listen to the sentences. Repeat them after the speaker, but substitute the appropriate verb plus particle plus preposition in place of the verb of the original sentence.*

1 2 3 4 5 6 7

C. **Verbs That Take Both *to* and *for* Plus an Indirect Object.** *Listen to the sentences and repeat them after the speaker.*

1 2 3 4 5 6

D. **Listening-Reading Response: True/False.** *Listen to the sentences. In your workbook read the two responses for each sentence. If the response is correct, circle* true *(T) in the answer column. If the answer is not correct, circle* false *(F). You will hear each sentence twice.*

   Example: Bob wrote a letter to Mary.

          a. Mary received a letter from Bob.   T F

          b. Someone else received Bob's letter.   T F

Sentence a *is true. Circle T in the answer column.*
Sentence b *is false. Circle F in the answer column.*

1. a. A secretary types letters instead of the boss.   T F

   b. A secretary types letters which she wants to give her boss.   T F

2. a. My father gave me money because he was renting an apartment from me.   T F

   b. My father paid money to my landlord instead of me.   T F

3. a. Mrs. Atkins taught an accounting class in place of three other teachers.   T F

   b. Mrs. Atkins had three other teachers as her students in accounting.   T F

4. a. Alan bought the bike.   T F

   b. Alan's bike was sold by John to someone else.   T F

Lesson 15

E. Adjective Plus Preposition. *Listen to the sentence and then the words or phrases that follow. Make a new sentence by combining these words or phrases with the original sentence. In doing so, you will need to use the appropriate preposition after the adjective.*

Example: The student was pleased. the results of the English test
The student was pleased at the results of the English test.

1 2 3 4 5 6 7 8

F. Summary Practice. *Listen to the short dialogues which you will hear twice. Repeat both parts of the dialogue after the second time.*

Example: Were you ever nervous about anything?
Of course I was. I was nervous about speaking in front of the class.
Were you ever nervous about anything?
Of course I was. I was nervous about speaking in front of the class.

1 2 3 4 5 6

Let's Practice II—The Verb *Wish*

A. *Listen to the questions and the answer cue that is given. Answer the questions using a complete sentence.*

Example: What do you wish to do tonight? visit my friends
I wish to visit my friends tonight.

1 2 3 4 5 6 7 8

B. Listening-Writing Response. *Listen to the sentences and questions which you will hear twice. After the second time repeat the response that is given and write it in your workbook.*

Example: Your next-door neighbors are never quiet. What do you wish?
I wish they were quiet.
Your next-door neighbors are never quiet. What do you wish?
I wish they were quiet.

1. _____

2. _____

3. _____

4. _____

Lesson 15

C. **Wishes for the Opposite.** *Listen to the sentences. If the statement is affirmative, make a wish in the negative. If the statement is negative, make a wish in the affirmative. Use the auxiliary verb in your response.*

   Examples: It's raining today.
   I wish it wasn't.
   I won't finish my work by three.
   I wish I would.

   1 2 3 4 5 6

D. *Listen to the sentences and respond by giving an affirmative sentence with* wish *and the cue word that is given.*

   Example: It's too bad the students failed the test. passed
   I wish the students had passed the test.

   1 2 3 4 5 6

E. **Summary Practice.** *Review wishes for the present, future, and past. Listen to the sentences and make a new sentence with* wish *and the appropriate auxiliary verb.*

   Examples: Bonnie doesn't like dogs.
   I wish she did.
   Henry is sick today.
   I wish he wasn't.
   My father won't send me any more money.
   I wish he would.
   Mother didn't cook dinner last night.
   I wish she had.

   1 2 3 4 5 6

F. **The Verb** *Hope.* *Listen to the sentences and answer the questions by using the cue words.*

   Example: You are going to try a new restaurant. What do you hope? the food will be good
   I hope the food will be good.

   1 2 3 4 5 6

Let's Practice III—Present and Past Participles as Adjectives and Past Participles as Adjective Complement after the Direct Object

A. *Listen to the sentences where the present participle occurs as an adjective and then make up a new sentence with the past participle of the same verb. Use* I *as the subject of the new sentence.*

   Example: The story was boring.
   I was bored.

   1 2 3 4 5 6 7 8

Lesson 15

B. *Listen to the sentences and choose the correct adjective in each case. Circle either the present or the past participle in your workbook.*

Example: I am   boring   bored   in this class.

Bored *is the correct answer. Circle* bored *in your workbook.*

1. depressing   depressed
2. depressing   depressed
3. interesting   interested
4. interesting   interested
5. amazing   amazed
6. tiring   tired

C. *Listen to the sentences and change them by using the past participle as an adjective complement after the direct object.*

Example: We had someone take our picture.
   We had our picture taken.

1   2   3   4

D. *Answer the question in a complete sentence by using the cue words given for you.*

Example: How long did it take you to get the motor started? fifteen minutes
   It took me fifteen minutes to get the motor started.

1   2   3   4

Let's Practice IV—The Passive Voice (Part 2) and Sentence Connectors: *Moreover, However, Therefore*

A. **Listening-Writing Response.** *Listen to the sentences as you read along in your workbook. Write in the complete verb forms that you hear.*

Example: They ___*saw*___ the boys at the movies. The boys ___*were seen*___ at the movies.

1. We _____ no message yet. No message _____ yet.

2. They _____ the old products. The old products _____.

3. They _____ us about the danger. We _____ about the danger.

4. They _____ the foreign students. The foreign students _____.

B. *Answer these questions in a complete sentence. The cue words will be given for you.*

Example: Do you know when the final exam in this course will be held? no
No, I don't know when the final exam in this course will be held.

1   2   3   4

C. Dictation. *Write the sentences after the speaker.*

1. _____

2. _____
   _____

3. _____
   _____

4. _____

Tape Script

Lesson 1: Asking for Information

Conversation

    Mrs. Foster: What's your name?
    Ali: Ali Hassan.
    Mrs. Foster: Where do you come from?
    Ali: I come from Jordan.
    Mrs. Foster: What language do you speak?
    Ali: I speak Arabic.
    Mrs. Foster: What do you do in Jordan?
    Ali: I'm an engineer.

(Answer Mrs. Foster.)

1. What's your name?
2. Where do you come from?
3. What language do you speak?
4. What do you do in your country?

Conversation

    Mrs. Foster: Where do you live?
    Ali: In Oak Park.
    Mrs. Foster: What's your address?
    Ali: It's 2567 East Waverly Avenue.
    Mrs. Foster: What's your telephone number?
    Ali: 578-2394.

(Answer the questions.)

1. Where do you live?
2. What's your address?
3. What's your telephone number?

Conversation

    Mrs. Foster: How long have you been here?
    Ali: I've been here since August 17.
    Mrs. Foster: How old are you?
    Ali: Twenty-one. I'm twenty-one years old.
    Mrs. Foster: When were you born?
    Ali: I was born on March 10.

(Answer the questions.)

1. How long have you been here?
2. How old are you?
3. When were you born?

Tape Script—Lesson 1

Conversation

Mrs. Foster: What are you studying now?
Ali: I'm studying English and engineering.
Mrs. Foster: What courses are you taking?
Ali: I'm taking English grammar and composition. I'm also taking two electrical engineering courses.
Mrs. Foster: How long have you been studying English?
Ali: For two years.

(Answer the questions.)

1. What are you studying now?
2. What courses are you taking?
3. How long have you been studying English?

Vocabulary Focus

1. Names

Bill: Hello. My name is William Henry Fraser. Please call me Bill.
Kato: I'm glad to meet you Bill. My name is Kato. My first name is Yukio.
Bill: Glad to know you Mr. Kato.

(Answer the question.)

1. What is William Henry Fraser's last name?
   His last name is Fraser.
2. What is Mr. Fraser's first name?
   His first name is William.
3. What is William's nickname?
   His nickname is Bill.
4. What is Yukio Kato's last name?
   His last name is Kato.
5. What is Mr. Kato's first name?
   His first name is Yukio.
6. What does Mr. Kato want to be called?
   He wants to be called Kato.

2. Titles of Address

3. Formal and Informal Introductions
Conversation: Formal Introduction

Mr. Brown: Ms. Stewart, I'd like you to meet my secretary, Ann Powers. Ann, Ms. Stewart is the new head of public relations.
Ms. Stewart: How do you do?
Ms. Powers: How do you do? I'm happy to meet you.

Conversation: Informal Introduction

Richard: Hello. My name is Richard Hastings.
Lucy: Glad to know you. I'm Lucy Brown.

Tape Script—Lesson 1

Conversation: Formal Greeting

Secretary: Good morning Ms. Stewart. How are you?
Boss: Fine, thank you. How are you?
Secretary: I'm fine too.

Informal Greeting

Richard: Hi, Lucy. How are you doing?
Lucy: O.K. And you?
Richard: Oh, pretty good.

Let's Practice I—Present Continuous Tense

A. Chen is a foreign student from China. He's standing in line at the English Institute with other foreign students. They're all waiting to register for English language courses. Chen has introduced himself to the girl in front of him. Her name is Rosita and she's from Mexico. Rosita is telling Chen that she's going to study English for one term and then take business courses at another university beginning in January. "What field are you in?" she asks Chen. Chen replies that he's in engineering. He's hoping to get his master's degree by the end of next summer.

Questions

1. Where is Chen standing in line?
   He's standing in line at the English Institute.
2. Who is standing in line with Chen?
   Other foreign students are standing in line with Chen.
3. What are the foreign students doing?
   They're waiting to register for English language courses.
4. Who is Chen talking to?
   He's talking to Rosita.
5. How long is Rosita going to study English?
   She's going to study English for one term.
6. Where is Rosita going to take business courses?
   She's going to take business courses at another university.
7. What is Chen studying?
   He's studying engineering.
8. When is he hoping to get his master's degree?
   He's hoping to get his master's degree by the end of next summer.

B. **Affirmative and Negative Sentences with *I* as Subject**

1. study   sleep.   I'm studying. I'm not sleeping.
2. listen   read.   I'm listening. I'm not reading.
3. practice   play.   I'm practicing. I'm not playing.
4. speak   write.   I'm speaking. I'm not writing.
5. work   walk.   I'm working. I'm not walking.
6. sit down   stand up.   I'm sitting down. I'm not standing up.

C. **Affirmative and Negative Sentences with *You* as Subject**

1. study   sleep.   You're studying. You aren't sleeping.
2. listen   read.   You're listening. You aren't reading.
3. practice   play.   You're practicing. You aren't playing.
4. speak   write.   You're speaking. You aren't writing.
5. work   walk.   You're working. You aren't walking.
6. sit down   stand up.   You're sitting down. You aren't standing up.

Tape Script—Lesson 1

D. Affirmative and Negative Sentences with *He* as Subject

1. study   sleep.   He's studying. He isn't sleeping.
2. listen   read.   He's listening. He isn't reading.
3. practice   play.   He's practicing. He isn't playing.
4. speak   write.   He's speaking. He isn't writing.
5. work   walk.   He's working. He isn't walking.
6. sit down   stand up.   He's sitting down. He isn't standing up.

E. *(Ask questions. Use the question word given in parentheses.)*

1. What are you asking the policeman?
2. Where are you going later?
3. What are you thinking about?
4. When is your friend arriving?
5. Who is Henry talking to?
6. How much money are the students paying for this course?
7. What time are we leaving?
8. Why are they buying a bigger house?

Let's Practice II—Simple Present Tense

A. *(Listen and repeat the sentences.)*

1. I work in a large company.
2. Frank works in a store.
3. We live in the suburbs.
4. Tom lives on Long Island.
5. You finish early every day.
6. Susan finishes work at three o'clock.

B. *(Listen and repeat these negative statements and questions.)*

1. I don't know the way to your house.
2. Bob doesn't know the way to your house.
3. Do you know the way to my house?
4. Does Bob know the way to my house?
5. They don't understand us.
6. Pedro doesn't understand us.
7. Do they understand the teacher?
8. Does Pedro understand the teacher?
9. You mean you're sorry.
10. Kim doesn't mean it.
11. What do you mean?
12. What does that mean?

C. What does a good student do?

1. watch TV all night. A good student doesn't watch TV all night.
2. do all his homework. A good student does all his homework.
3. practice English daily. A good student practices English daily.
4. sleep in class. A good student doesn't sleep in class.
5. miss class. A good student doesn't miss class.
6. pay attention to the teacher. A good student pays attention to the teacher.
7. lose her notes. A good student doesn't lose her notes.
8. have a pen and paper with him. A good student has a pen and paper with him.

Let's Practice III—Present Perfect Tense (Part 1)

A. *(Listen and repeat.)*

1. I have lived in this country for three years.
2. John has worked for his father since 1981.
3. You have traveled around the world.
4. Mrs. Smith has started a new job.
5. They have given me a lot of help.
6. Mary has run in a lot of races.
7. I have been sick for two weeks.
8. Ricardo has had his motorcycle since October.

B. *(Listen and repeat.)*

1. Jenny has been practicing the flute for an hour.
2. The children have been watching TV for a long time.
3. It has been raining since yesterday.
4. I have been trying to learn English since last year.
5. We have been waiting for the bus for twenty minutes.
6. Tom has been doing his homework all afternoon.

C. Questions and Answers with *How Long*

1. How long have you been in this country?
   I have been here for one month.
2. How long have you been living in this town?
   I have been living in this town since January.
3. How long has Mohammed been studying English?
   He has been studying English for almost one year.
4. How long have we been waiting?
   We have been waiting for over an hour.
5. How long have you played the guitar?
   I have played the guitar since I was fifteen.
6. How long has Ken worked here?
   He has worked here since last month.

D. Listening-Writing Response

1. How long have you been in this country?
2. How long have you been living in this town?
3. How long have you been studying English?
4. How long have you had your passport?

E. Dictation

1. The students are learning English.
2. Do you understand what you hear on the tape?
3. We have been sitting here for half an hour.
4. My friend likes tea but he doesn't like coffee.

End of lesson 1

Lesson 2: Reporting the Facts

Conversation

A. The Great Bank Robbery

Reporter: What happened?
Miss Lee: The bank was robbed.
Reporter: Which bank was it?
Miss Lee First National Bank.
Reporter: When did it happen?
Miss Lee: About fifteen minutes ago.
Reporter: Who did it?
Miss Lee: I don't know. A bad guy. He was wearing a mask.
Reporter: How did he do it?
Miss Lee: He threatened the teller with a gun.
Reporter: How did he get away?
Miss Lee: He escaped through the back door.
Reporter: How much money was stolen?
Miss Lee: Someone said over $100,000.
Reporter: Was anyone hurt?
Miss Lee: I don't think so, but the thief fired two shots into the air before he left.

B. Listening-Writing Response. *(Refer to conversation A above.)*

Vocabulary Focus

1. Banking Terms *(See lesson 2, page 9.)*

2. The Verbs *Borrow* and *Lend*
A. *(Listen and repeat.)*

   1. May I borrow your pen?
   2. Could I please borrow your car?
   3. I need to borrow a cup of sugar.
   4. The student borrowed a book.
   5. She borrowed a book from the teacher.
   6. Henry borrowed five dollars.
   7. He borrowed five dollars from his brother.

B. *(Listen and repeat.)*

   1. Can you lend me a piece of paper?
   2. Would you please lend me twenty-five cents?
   3. Will you lend me some sugar?
   4. The teacher lent me a book.
   5. The teacher lent a book to me.
   6. The bank will lend you money.
   7. The bank will lend money to you.

C. Borrow versus Lend

1. Tom needed another stamp. He asked his friend Paul to   borrow (lend) him one.
2. Linda didn't have enough flour to bake bread. She (borrowed) lent   some from her neighbor.
3. Could you   borrow (lend) me fifty dollars? I'll pay you back next week.
4. May I (borrow) lend   your English book? I can't find mine.
5. Fred (borrowed) lent   eight dollars from his brother.
6. Would you please   borrow (lend) me your eraser?
7. Banks will   borrow (lend) you money but you have to pay interest on the amount you (borrow) lend.

Let's Practice I—Simple Past Tense

A. Regular Verbs. *(See lesson 2, page 10.)*

B. *(See lesson 2, page 10.)*

C. *(See lesson 2, page 10.)*

D. *(Write the verbs in the blank spaces. The verbs are given in italics.)*

1. John *wrote* a letter to his sister, but she *didn't get* it.
2. Mr. Brown *didn't think* I *knew* the answer but I *did*.
3. Mr. Thompson *left* town and he never *came* back.
4. I *made* only two mistakes on the test.
5. My brother *took* my book because he *thought* I *didn't want* it anymore.

E. Questions

1. I went somewhere yesterday. Where?
   Where did you go?
2. I went to the bank. What time?
   What time did you go to the bank?
3. I spoke to someone at the bank. Who?
   Who did you speak to?
4. I asked her a question. Why?
   Why did you ask her a question?
5. I needed to know something. What?
   What did you need to know?
6. I borrowed a lot of money yesterday. How much?
   How much money did you borrow?

Tape Script—Lesson 2

Let's Practice II—Past Continuous Tense

A. **Answering Questions**

1. What were you doing in the library? read a book
   I was reading a book.
2. What were you doing in the kitchen? make dinner
   I was making dinner.
3. What was Mary doing in the park? take a walk
   She was taking a walk.
4. Where was Charles going this morning? to work
   He was going to work.
5. What was Jack growing in his garden? tomatoes and lettuce
   He was growing tomatoes and lettuce in his garden.
6. When was the boy sleeping? all afternoon
   He was sleeping all afternoon.

B. **Listening Comprehension**

Jenny was sitting in the living room. She was watching TV. She was watching a police show. Jenny didn't really like it because there was too much violence. Everybody was shooting everybody else. Two of the bad guys were trying to kill one of the good guys. But the police came just in time to save him. Suddenly the program stopped and an announcer began to give a commercial about deodorants. He was comparing the effectiveness of two famous brands. Jenny was still thinking about the police story and wasn't paying any attention to the advertisement. She wondered why she was wasting her time in front of the TV.

Questions

1. Where was Jenny sitting?
   She was sitting in the living room.
2. What was she doing?
   She was watching TV.
3. Did Jenny like the police show?
   No, she didn't.
4. Why didn't she like the police show?
   Because there was too much violence.
5. Why did the program stop?
   Because an announcer began to give a commercial about deodorants.
6. What was the announcer comparing?
   He was comparing the effectiveness of two famous brands of deodorants.
7. Why wasn't Jenny paying any attention to the commercial?
   Because she was still thinking about the police story.
8. Did Jenny think she was making good use of her time by watching TV?
   No, she thought she was wasting her time by watching TV.

C. *Used To*

1. Where did you use to live when you were young?
   I used to live in El Paso, Texas when I was young.
2. What did you use to do when you were a child?
   I used to play football and baseball when I was a child.
3. What kind of food did your family use to eat?
   We used to eat Mexican food. We used to have lots of beans and corn.
4. What kind of books did you use to read when you were young?
   I used to read animal stories when I was young.
5. Where did your family use to go on vacation when you lived in Texas?
   We used to go to Mexico to visit our relatives there.

D. Listening-Writing Response

1. Where did you use to live when you were young?
2. What did you use to do when you were a child?
3. What kind of food did your family use to eat?
4. What kind of books did you use to read when you were young?
5. Where did your family use to go on vacation when you lived in your country?

Let's Practice III—Emphatic *Do, Does, Did*

Indeed I do.

1. Do you miss your family?
   Yes, indeed. I do miss my family.
2. Do you prefer the food from your country?
   Yes, indeed. I do prefer the food from my country.
3. Does your teacher speak good English?
   Yes, indeed. My teacher does speak good English.
4. Do you have a valid passport?
   Yes, indeed. I do have a valid passport.
5. Did you get a student visa?
   Yes, indeed. I did get a student visa.
6. Did you think the English test was difficult?
   Yes, indeed. I did think the English test was difficult.

Let's Practice IV—The Passive Voice (Part 1)

A. Incomplete Dialogue

1. First National Bank was robbed.
2. It was robbed about ten thirty in the morning.
3. Over one hundred thousand dollars were stolen.
4. The teller was threatened with a gun.
5. Two shots were fired.
6. No, the teller wasn't killed.
7. No, no one was hurt.
8. The robbery was reported to the police ten minutes later.

Tape Script—Lesson 2

B. Passive Voice

1. Where are camels found?
   Camels are found in the dessert.
2. Where are deer found?
   Deer are found in the woods.
3. Where are lions found?
   Lions are found in Africa.
4. Where are mosquitos found?
   Mosquitos are found in swamps.
5. Where are flies found?
   Flies are found everywhere.
6. Where is the Eiffel Tower located?
   The Eiffel Tower is located in Paris, France.
7. Where is the White House located?
   The White House is located in Washington, D.C.
8. Where are movies made in the United States?
   Movies are made in Hollywood.
9. In what century was the telephone invented?
   The telephone was invented in the nineteenth century.
10. In what century was the airplane invented?
    The airplane was invented in the twentieth century.
11. When was America discovered?
    America was discovered in 1492.
12. By whom was America discovered?
    America was discovered by Christopher Columbus.

C. Dictation

1. The boy was late for school because he overslept this morning.
2. Tom used to have a lot of friends when he was living in New York.
3. Teachers do like good students and students do like good teachers.

End of lesson 2

Lesson 3: What's the Weather Like?

Conversation

What Season Is It?

1. It's spring. It's raining. The girl is carrying an umbrella.
2. It's summer. It's sunny and hot. The girl is sunbathing.
3. It's fall. It's cool and windy. The boy is raking leaves.
4. It's winter. It's cold. It's snowing. The children are making a snowman.

Vocabulary Focus

A. Weather and Climate Expressions

It is hot.	It's fair.	It's foggy.
It is warm.	It's nice.	It's stormy.
It's cool.	It's mild.	It's terrible.
It's chilly.	It's cloudy.	It's dry.
It's cold.	It's windy.	It's humid.
It's freezing.	It's raining.	It's wet.
It's sunny out.	It's snowing.	It's icy.

Climates	*Seasons*	*Bad Storms*
hot	spring	tornado
cold	summer	hurricane
tropical	fall	flood
semitropical	winter	typhoon
temperate	dry	earthquake
frigid	rainy	

B. Listening Comprehension

The Climate of North America

The climate of North America varies from tropical to frigid. Certain parts of Mexico, and the Everglades of Florida are tropical. The frigid regions are found in parts of Alaska and northern Canada. Most of the United States and the populated areas of Canada have hot or warm weather in the summer and cold weather in the winter. In the spring, the weather is usually warm and pleasant. It often rains in the spring too.

Questions

1. What is the climate like in North America?
2. What is the weather like in the summer?
3. What is the weather like in the winter?
4. What is the weather like in the spring?
5. When does it often rain?

(Answers)

1. The climate in North America varies from tropical to frigid.
2. The weather is mostly hot or warm in the summer.
3. The weather is mostly cold in the winter.
4. The weather is usually warm and pleasant in the spring.

Tape Script—Lesson 3

C. *(The Climate of North America Continued)*
Listen to the rest of the passage and the questions. There are five questions in this part.

The Climate of North America Continued

In the fall the days grow shorter and the weather turns cool. It snows in the North and Midwest of the United States and in Canada in the winter. In the South of the United States and on the West Coast, the winters are usually mild. Some regions, such as the East Coast and the Great Lakes States, are very hot and humid in the summer. Other regions, such as the Southwest, are always hot and dry.

Questions

1. What is the weather like in the fall?
2. Where does it snow in the winter?
3. Where are the winters usually mild?
4. What regions are hot and humid in the summer?
5. What region is always hot and dry?

(Answers)

1. The weather turns cool in the fall.
2. It snows in the North and Midwest of the United States and Canada in the winter.
3. The winters are usually mild in the South of the United States and on the West Coast.
4. The East Coast and the Great Lakes States are hot and humid in the summer.
5. The Southwest is always hot and dry.

Let's Practice I—Single-Word Adverbs of Frequency

A.
1. It always snows in Denver in December.
2. It usually snows in Chicago in December.
3. It often snows in New York in December.
4. It sometimes snows in St. Louis in December.
5. It rarely snows in Seattle in December.
6. It never snows in San Diego in December.
7. It is never cold in Honolulu in the winter.
8. It is usually cold in San Francisco in the winter.
9. It is often cold in Little Rock in the winter.
10. It is always cold in Minneapolis in the winter.

B.
1. Does it usually snow in Chicago in December? Yes, usually
   Yes, it usually snows in Chicago in December.
2. Does it ever snow in San Diego in December? No, never
   No, it never snows in San Diego in December.
3. Does it often rain in Seattle in the winter? Yes, often
   Yes, it often rains in Seattle in the winter.
4. Does it sometimes snow in St. Louis in the winter? Yes, sometimes
   Yes, it sometimes snows in St. Louis in the winter.
5. Is it ever cold in Minneapolis in the winter? Yes, always
   Yes, it's always cold in Minneapolis in the winter.
6. Is it usually warm in San Francisco in the winter? No, not usually
   No, it's not usually warm in San Francisco in the winter.
7. Is it ever hot in Denver in December? No, never
   No, it's never hot in Denver in December.
8. Is it usually cold in Houston in the winter? No, rarely
   No, it's rarely cold in Houston in the winter.

Let's Practice II—*How Often* and *How Long*

A. 1. How often do you see Bob?
    I see him once a month.
    2. How often do you play tennis?
    I usually play tennis three times a week.
    3. How often does the mail come?
    The mail comes once a day, five days a week.
    4. How long does school last?
    School lasts from eight in the morning to three in the afternoon.
    5. How long have you been in this country?
    I've been here for three years.
    6. How long will the concert last?
    It will last approximately two hours.

B. **Listening-Writing Response**

    1. How often do you see Bob?
    2. How often do you play tennis?
    3. How often does the mail come?
    4. How long does school last?
    5. How long have you been in this country?
    6. How long will the concert last?

C. **Richard's Schedule**

    1. How often does Richard's French class meet?
    His French class meets four days a week.
    2. How often does Richard's economics class meet?
    His economics class meets three days a week.
    3. How often does Richard's chemistry lecture meet?
    His chemistry lecture meets three days a week.
    4. How often does his chem lab meet?
    His chem lab meets twice a week.
    5. How long does Richard's English class last?
    His English class lasts one hour.
    6. How long does his physical education class last?
    His physical education class lasts two hours.
    7. When does he go to the language lab?
    He goes to the language lab on Tuesdays and Thursdays from ten to eleven.
    8. What days of the week does he have off?
    He has Saturdays and Sundays off.

Let's Practice III—*There Is* and *There Are*

A. 1. A bird is singing in the tree.
    There's a bird singing in the tree.
    2. A cat was watching the bird.
    There was a cat watching the bird.
    3. Many people were in the park yesterday.
    There were many people in the park yesterday.

Tape Script—Lesson 3

    4. Tickets are available for the concert tonight.
       There are tickets available for the concert tonight.
    5. An old man was walking down the street.
       There was an old man walking down the street.
    6. Eleven players are on a soccer team.
       There are eleven players on a soccer team.

B. 1. There aren't any tickets left for the show.
       There are no tickets left for the show.
    2. There aren't any parking places left.
       There are no parking places left.
    3. There weren't any boats in the river yesterday.
       There were no boats in the river yesterday.
    4. There weren't any clouds in the sky this morning.
       There were no clouds in the sky this morning.
    5. There isn't any water in the canteen.
       There's no water in the canteen.
    6. There wasn't any mail for you.
       There was no mail for you.
    7. There isn't any more blue paint left.
       There's no more blue paint left.
    8. There wasn't any more hope left.
       There was no more hope left.

Let's Practice IV—Future Time

A.   **Listening Comprehension**

Plans for the Summer

     Lisa and Frank Baxter are planning to take a trip to the West of the United States next summer. They're discussing their itinerary now so they know where they're going to go and what they're going to see. First they're going to leave from Chicago and head west toward Denver. Denver is in the Rocky Mountains. After Denver they'll drive north to see the natural wonders of Yellowstone National Park in Wyoming.

Questions

1. What are the Baxters going to do next summer?
2. What are they discussing now?
3. What city will they leave from?
4. What city will they visit first?
5. Where are they going to go in Wyoming?

(Answers)

1. The Baxters are going to take a trip to the West of the United States next summer.
2. They're discussing their itinerary now.
3. They will leave from Chicago.
4. They will visit Denver first.
5. They're going to go to Yellowstone National Park.

B. Plans for the Summer Continued

They intend to spend about a week camping in the park and then they'll go on to Salt Lake City, Utah. Their next stop is Las Vegas, Nevada, where they're going to spend their money in the gambling casinos. Will they win or lose money in Las Vegas? Even if they are lucky, they probably won't win very much. Finally, Lisa and Frank are going to reach California. They're going to travel along the Pacific coast on Route 1 and enjoy the beautiful scenery.

Questions

1. How long will they stay in Yellowstone National Park?
2. After that where are they going to go?
3. Where are they going to gamble?
4. Do they expect to win a lot of money?
5. Where are they going to travel in California?

(Answers)

1. They'll stay about a week in the park.
2. After that they'll go on to Salt Lake City, Utah.
3. They're going to gamble in Las Vegas, Nevada.
4. No, they don't expect to win a lot of money.
5. They're going to travel along the Pacific coast on Route 1.

C. Questions with *Be Going To*

1. finish your work; when
   When are you going to finish your work?
2. watch TV; when
   When are you going to watch TV?
3. visit tomorrow; who
   Who are you going to visit tomorrow?
4. go next weekend; where
   Where are you going to go next weekend?
5. do tonight; what
   What are you going to do tonight?
6. live next year; where
   Where are you going to live next year?

D. Questions with *Will*

1. eat for dinner tonight; what
   What will you eat for dinner tonight?
2. learn English well; when
   When will you learn English well?
3. go to Los Angeles; how
   How will you go to Los Angeles?
4. invite to the party; who
   Who will you invite to the party?
5. get to the airport; how
   How will you get to the airport?
6. get married; when
   When will you get married?

Tape Script—Lesson 3

E. Promises

1. I promise to write you every day.
   I'll write you every day.
2. I promise to pay you back next week.
   I'll pay you back next week.
3. We promise to visit you soon.
   We'll visit you soon.
4. I promise never to forget you.
   I'll never forget you.
5. I promise never to be afraid.
   I'll never be afraid.
6. We promise not make any mistakes.
   We won't make any mistakes.

F. Listening-Writing Response

The first weather report: The weather will be cloudy and cold tomorrow. There is likely to be some precipitation, and possibly it will snow if the temperature remains low.

Questions

1. Will it be sunny tomorrow?
   No, it won't.
2. Will it be cold tomorrow?
   Yes, it will.
3. Will it be dry?
   No, it won't.
4. Will it snow if the temperature remains low?
   Yes, it will.

The second weather report: The weather will be hot and humid tomorrow with the temperature in the high eighties. It will be sunny most of the day, but a storm which is currently over the Rocky Mountains will reach us by late afternoon.

Questions

1. Will the weather be hot tomorrow?
   Yes, it will.
2. Will it be sunny all day long?
   No, it won't.
3. Will the storm come from the Smoky Mountains?
   No, it won't.
4. Will the storm reach us by late afternoon?
   Yes, it will.

G. Dictation

1. Mary won't be coming home until next week.
2. How often do you go shopping?
3. There aren't any more tickets left for the concert.

End of lesson 3

Lesson 4: Have You Heard the News?

Conversation

A. The Latest Gossip

Kathy: Have you heard the latest?
Phil: No, I haven't. I've been away all summer.
Kathy: Christine Kelly, the millionaire's daughter eloped with her tennis coach.
Phil: Really! When?
Kathy: Last week. Her parents are furious.
Phil: Well, it's her life. Let her choose her own husband.

B. I'm sorry to hear about it.

Tom: Have you heard about Mrs. Murphy who fell down the stairs and broke her leg?
Julie: No, I haven't. That's terrible. What else has happened since I left town?
Tom: My next-door neighbor Mr. Farrell had a heart attack and is in the hospital. You know he's been sick for two years now.
Julie: That's too bad. I'm sorry to hear about it.

Vocabulary Focus

Have Got

A. 1. I have got a new car. I've got a new car.
    2. We have got some friends here. We've got some friends here.
    3. You have got to help me. You've got to help me.
    4. Mary has got a new teacher. Mary's got a new teacher.
    5. She has got to work hard. She's got to work hard.
    6. They have not got much time. They haven't got much time.
    7. John has not got any change. He hasn't got any change.

B. 1. What have you got in your pocket?
       I've got a wallet, a comb, and a handkerchief.
    2. What has the teacher got on her desk?
       She's got books and papers on her desk.
    3. Have you got a cigarette?
       No, I haven't. I don't smoke.
    4. What have you got to do this evening?
       I've got to study for my history test.
    5. What has Tim got to do every day?
       Tim's got to go to school every day.
    6. Why have you got to listen to these tapes?
       I've got to learn English well.

Let's Practice I—Relative Clauses (Part 1)

A. 1. I know the man. The man is standing on the corner. who
       I know the man who is standing on the corner.
    2. I see the woman. She is wearing a red coat. who
       I see the woman who is wearing a red coat.
    3. I take the train. It leaves at eight o'clock. which
       I take the train which leaves at eight o'clock.
    4. We want the room. The room faces the garden. which
       We want the room which faces the garden.

Tape Script—Lesson 4

    5. Bob has many friends. They are very rich. that
       Bob has many friends that are very rich.
    6. Chicago is a city. It has some of the tallest buildings in the world. that
       Chicago is a city that has some of the tallest buildings in the world.

B.   1. The instructor taught our class. He moved to Oklahoma. who
       The instructor who taught our class moved to Oklahoma.
    2. The high school is in El Paso. It is new and modern. that
       The high school that is in El Paso is new and modern.
    3. The child has a red balloon. He's my nephew. that
       The child that has a red balloon is my nephew.
    4. The dog bit me. The dog belongs to Mr. Jones. which
       The dog which bit me belongs to Mr. Jones.

C.   1. I didn't know the doctor. His son is in Jane's class.
       I didn't know the doctor whose son is in Jane's class.
    2. The teacher praised the girl. Her paper was the best in the class.
       The teacher praised the girl whose paper was the best in the class.
    3. Detroit is a city. Its population is decreasing.
       Detroit is a city whose population is decreasing.
    4. The man's parents came from Mexico. The man works in the store.
       The man whose parents came from Mexico works in the store.
    5. The car's engine was brand new. The car was running well.
       The car's whose engine was brand new was running well.

Let's Practice II—Present Perfect Tense (Part 2)

A.   1. I have been sick. I've been sick.
    2. You have been away for a long time. You've been away for a long time.
    3. We have finished our work. We've finished our work.
    4. They have studied all week. They've studied all week.
    5. John has tried that restaurant. John's tried that restaurant.
    6. He has eaten there several times. He's eaten there several times.
    7. The food has always been good. The food's always been good.
    8. We have not been here long. We haven't been here long.
    9. Jane has not left for school yet. Jane hasn't left for school yet.
  10. She has not done all her homework. She hasn't done all her homework.

B.   1. What have you been doing in the language laboratory?
       I've been listening to English tapes.
    2. What have you been reading?
       I've been reading the newspaper.
    3. Who has John been talking to?
       He's been talking to his teacher.
    4. What has Mary been doing after class?
       She's been studying in the library.
    5. Where have your friends been going at night?
       They've been going to the movies at night.

C.
1. What have you been doing in the language laboratory?
   I've been listening to English tapes.
   What have you been doing in the language laboratory?
2. What have you been reading?
   I've been reading the newspaper.
   What have you been reading?
3. Who has John been talking to?
   He's been talking to his teacher.
   Who has John been talking to?
4. What has Mary been doing after class?
   She's been studying in the library.
   What has Mary been doing after class?
5. Where have your friends been going at night?
   They've been going to the movies.
   Where have your friends been going at night?

D.
1. Mary has been on a diet. How long
   How long has Mary been on a diet?
2. I've been reading. What
   What have you been reading?
3. I haven't been feeling well. How long
   How long haven't you been feeling well?
4. My sister hasn't been eating dessert anymore. Why
   Why hasn't your sister been eating dessert anymore?
5. Bob's been going to the library. When
   When has Bob been going to the library?
6. He's been riding his bicycle. Where
   Where has he been riding his bicycle?

Let's Practice III—Time Expressions Used with the Present Perfect and Simple Past Tenses

A.
1. Susan has been studying computer science. She has taken courses for two semesters so far. She started last September.

   What has Susan been studying?
   She's been studying computer science.
   How long has she taken courses?
   She's taken courses for two semesters so far.
   When did she start her computer science courses?
   She started her computer science courses last September.

2. Chen has been in the kitchen since five-thirty. He's been preparing a Chinese dinner for his friends. It's seven o'clock now and he has finally finished cooking.

   How long has Chen been in the kitchen?
   He's been in the kitchen since five-thirty.
   Why has Chen been in the kitchen so long?
   He's been preparing a Chinese dinner for his friends.
   Has he finished cooking yet?
   Yes, he's finally finished cooking.
   What time did he finish?
   He finished at seven o'clock.

Tape Script—Lesson 4

3. Charles and Lisa got married last August. They have been married for six months. They have been thinking about buying a house but they haven't found one yet that they can afford.

   When did Charles and Lisa get married?
   They got married last August.
   How long have they been married?
   They've been married for six months.
   What have they been thinking about buying?
   They've been thinking about buying a house.
   Why haven't they bought a house yet?
   They haven't found one that they can afford.

4. Mr. and Mrs. Perez have never been to South America. They have been meaning to visit South America for the past ten years, but so far they have never had enough time or money to go.

   Where have Mr. and Mrs. Perez never been?
   Mr. and Mrs. Perez have never been to South America.
   How long have they been meaning to visit South America?
   They've been meaning to visit South America for the past ten years.
   Have they saved up enough money for the trip?
   No, they haven't saved up enough money for the trip.

B. 1. How long have you known your teacher? since the beginning of the course
    I've known my teacher since the beginning of the course.
    2. How long have you been studying English? for several years
    I've been studying English for several years.
    3. How many years has Pedro been in the United States. for five years
    He has been in the United States for five years.
    4. How many hours have the children been watching TV? for two hours
    They've been watching TV for two hours.
    5. How long has Mohammed been married? since 1981
    He's been married since 1981.
    6. How long has Gloria had her own apartment? for three months
    She has had her own apartment for three months.

C. 1. Do you want to go to Toronto? be
    I've already been to Toronto.
    2. Do you want to talk to Mrs. Ramsey? speak
    I've already spoken to Mrs. Ramsey.
    3. Shall I introduce you to Paul? meet
    I've already met Paul.
    4. Did you begin dinner yet? make
    I've already made it.
    5. Shall I repair your TV? fix
    I've already fixed my TV.
    6. Will you please write him? telephone
    I've already telephoned him.

Tape Script—Lesson 4

D. 1. get dressed
       Have you gotten dressed yet?
    2. eat breakfast
       Have you eaten breakfast yet?
    3. do your homework
       Have you done your homework yet?
    4. drink your tea
       Have you drunk your tea yet?
    5. go to Niagara Falls
       Have you gone to Niagara Falls yet?
    6. buy a house
       Have you bought a house yet?
    7. write to your family
       Have you written to your family yet?
    8. visit your friends
       Have you visited your friends yet?

E. 1. Are you standing up now? No
       No, I'm not.
    2. Will you see me tomorrow? Yes
       Yes, I will.
    3. Would you like to meet Mary? Yes
       Yes, I would.
    4. Have you ever been to the moon? No
       No, I haven't.
    5. Is the teacher eating dinner now? No
       No, she isn't.
    6. Have you been paying attention to the lesson? Yes
       Yes, I have.
    7. Were your friends at the concert? No
       No, they weren't.
    8. Does Bob have to go now? Yes
       Yes, he does.
    9. Did we finish lesson 3 yet? Yes
       Yes, we did.
   10. Has Henry been attending class regularly? No
       No, he hasn't.
   11. Can you swim? Yes
       Yes, I can.
   12. Are the students crying? No
       No, they aren't.
   13. Have we practiced enough? No
       No, we haven't.
   14. Has Susan ever been married? Yes
       Yes, she has.
   15. Does Tom's sister know how to drive? Yes
       Yes, she does.

F. **Dictation**

    1. The sky has gotten darker and the weather has become cooler.
    2. The weather bureau has been predicting a storm for this afternoon.
    3. Have you heard that Mrs. Gomez fell on the ice and broke her wrist?
    4. The car whose engine is brand new has been running very well now.

End of lesson 4

Lesson 5: Aches and Pains

Conversation

A. At the Doctor's

Doctor: Tell me what's wrong.
Patient: I don't feel very well. I'm dizzy and a little feverish. I've got a sore throat, a runny nose, and my muscles ache.
Doctor: It sounds like the flu or a bad cold. Stay in bed, drink plenty of liquids, and take aspirin every four hours.

B. Where does it Hurt?

Doctor: Where does it hurt?
Patient: Here. I've got a pain in my chest.
Doctor: Does it hurt here too?
Patient: No, not there. Just in my chest.

Vocabulary Focus

1. Expressions of Aches and Pains

   1. I've got a headache.
   2. I've got a toothache.
   3. I've got an earache.
   4. I've got a stomachache.
   5. I've got a backache.
   6. I've got a sore foot.
   7. I've got a sore toe.
   8. I've got a sore hand.
   9. I've got a sore muscle.
   10. I've got a sore throat.

2. Being Sick or Injured

   1. I feel sick today.
   2. I feel ill.
   3. I don't feel very well.
   4. I caught a cold.
   5. I have the flu.
   6. I feel dizzy.
   7. I'm hot.
   8. I'm feverish.
   9. I have a fever.
   10. I'm cold.
   11. I'm shivering.
   12. I'm trembling.
   13. I feel faint.
   14. I feel sick to my stomach.
   15. I fainted.
   16. I threw up.
   17. I'm coughing.
   18. I'm sneezing.
   19. I have a cough.
   20. I have a runny nose.
   21. I got hurt.
   22. I sprained my ankle.
   23. I have a sprained ankle.
   24. I pulled a muscle.
   25. I have a pulled muscle.
   26. I have an injury.
   27. I was injured.
   28. I injured my back.
   29. I broke my leg.
   30. I have a broken leg.

3. What does a doctor do? What does a nurse do?

   1. A doctor treats patients.
   2. A doctor examines patients.
   3. A doctor takes your blood pressure.
   4. A doctor listens to your heart with a stethoscope.
   5. A doctor prescribes medicine.
   6. A doctor performs operations.
   7. A nurse assists the doctor.
   8. A nurse takes your temperature with a thermometer.
   9. A nurse takes your pulse.
   10. A nurse takes blood samples.
   11. A nurse gives injections with a syringe.

4. True or False
   Example: 1. True 2. False

   1. If you have a toothache, you should see the dentist. True
   2. If you are feeling good, the doctor will prescribe some medicine for you. False
   3. If you are throwing up, you should eat more food. False
   4. If you have a fever, you should drink a lot of liquids. True
   5. If you've got a bad cough, you should kiss your girlfriend or boyfriend. False
   6. When the doctor listens to your heart, he uses a stethoscope. True
   7. The job of a nurse is to help the doctor. True
   8. When you have a sprained ankle, you should walk on that foot. False

Let's Practice I—Noun Modifiers

A. 1. The waiter dropped his tray. He was clumsy and careless.
       The clumsy, careless waiter dropped his tray.
    2. My friends bought a house. It was new, large, and modern.
       My friends bought a new large modern house.
    3. The animal was looking for food. The animal was cold and frightened.
       The cold frightened animal was looking for food.
    4. I read a book. It was long and interesting.
       I read a long interesting book.
    5. I didn't like that medicine. That medicine was awful tasting.
       I didn't like that awful tasting medicine.
    6. The air felt good. It was cool and fresh.
       The cool fresh air felt good.

B. 1. The nurse will help you. The nurse is by the door.
       The nurse by the door will help you.
    2. The hospital is on Huron Street. It was built fifty years ago.
       The hospital on Huron Street was built fifty years ago.
    3. The man wants to see you. He is in the hall.
       The man in the hall wants to see you.
    4. We found a restaurant. It was near the station.
       We found a restaurant near the station.
    5. Isabel's father owns a store. It's in Miami.
       Isabel's father owns a store in Miami.
    6. We had to cut down the tree. It was in front of the house.
       We had to cut down the tree in front of the house.

Tape Script—Lesson 5

C.
1. The animal is a cat. It is climbing a tree.
   The animal climbing a tree is a cat.
2. The person is a nurse. The person is wearing a uniform.
   The person wearing a uniform is a nurse.
3. I didn't recognize the man. He was sitting by the window.
   I didn't recognize the man sitting by the window.
4. The people searched for the treasure. The treasure was hidden.
   The people searched for the hidden treasure.
5. The child cried for her mother. She was frightened.
   The frightened child cried for her mother.
6. The student didn't come to class. He was tired.
   The tired student didn't come to class.

D.
1. George wrecked his car. He had just repaired it.
   George wrecked his car which he had just repaired.
2. Mexico is a country. I have visited it.
   Mexico is a country which I have visited.
3. Do you like the book? You have to read it.
   Do you like the book which you have to read?
4. I don't know of anyone. You can ask anyone.
   I don't know of anyone whom you can ask.
5. There is the teacher. We had her last year.
   There is the teacher whom we had last year.
6. Where are the children? She was taking care of them.
   Where are the children whom she was taking care of?

E.
1. There is the woman. Her suitcase was stolen.
   There is the woman whose suitcase was stolen.
2. There is the man. We met his daughter yesterday.
   There is the man whose daughter we met yesterday.
3. Do you know the people? Their children were playing by the river.
   Do you know the people whose children were playing by the river?
4. Detroit is a city. Its population is decreasing.
   Detroit is a city whose population is decreasing.
5. Houston is a city. Its population is increasing.
   Houston is a city whose population is increasing.
6. Do you go to the school? Its football team won the state championship.
   Do you go to the school whose football team won the state championship?

F.
1. I have been to the city. Tony comes from that city.
   I know the city where Tony comes from.
2. Do you know the date? Ali will get here on that date.
   Do you know the date when Ali will get here?
3. This is the house. We live in this house.
   This is the house where we live.
4. There is the restaurant. Our class will meet for lunch at that restaurant.
   There is the restaurant where our class will meet for lunch.
5. George doesn't know the year. He will finish his degree that year.
   George doesn't know when he will finish his degree.
6. Yesterday was the day. They said they were coming yesterday.
   Yesterday was the day when they said they were coming.

Tape Script—Lesson 5

G.   Listening-Reading Response

1. Bob hasn't met the doctor yet who will perform surgery on his knee.   a. T   b. F
2. The village where I was born was so small it wasn't even on the map.   a. F   b. T
3. Steve forgot the name of the teacher whom his friend had for computer science.   a. F   b. T
4. The boy whose dog won first place in the dog show also won first prize in a mathematics contest.   a. T   b. T
5. Mary fell in love with a French soldier who had to go back to his country.   a. F   b. T
6. The man whose grown son just wrecked the family car is a good friend of Dr. Kelsey.   a. F   b. F

Let's Practice II—Adverbs of Manner

A. 1. The people are patient. are waiting
       The people are waiting patiently.
    2. The young horse is awkward. is walking
       The young horse is walking awkwardly.
    3. We were slow. were walking
       We were walking slowly.
    4. The doctor was frank. spoke
       The doctor spoke frankly.
    5. My boss was evasive. answered
       My boss answered evasively.
    6. They were fast. ran
       They ran fast.
    7. The airplane was low in the sky. flew
       The airplane flew low in the sky.
    8. The road is straight. goes
       The road goes straight.
    9. The train is never punctual. never arrives
       The train never arrives punctually.
   10. Mark is good. sings
       Mark sings well.
   11. Mary was happy. was working
       Mary was working happily.
   12. The team was enthusiastic. played
       The team played enthusiastically.

B. 1. Does a race car move fast or slowly?
       A race car moves fast.
    2. Does a jet plane fly low or high?
       A jet plane flies high.
    3. Should you speak honestly or dishonestly to your parents?
       You should speak honestly to your parents.
    4. Does a person who sings out of tune sing well or badly?
       A person who sings out of tune sings badly.
    5. Do your teachers usually speak intelligently or stupidly?
       My teachers usually speak intelligently.
    6. Does a surgeon use his hands skillfully or unskillfully?
       A surgeon uses his hands skillfully.
    7. Does a dancer move awkwardly or gracefully?
       A dancer moves gracefully.

Tape Script—Lesson 5

Let's Practice III—Word Order in Sentences

    Example: Mary (S) threw (V) the ball (O).

1. The train (S) left (V).
2. It (S) was raining (V).
3. The cat (S) caught (V) a mouse (O).
4. Tom (S) will write (V) a letter (O).
5. We (S) can't forget (V) our passports (O).
6. The students (S) were playing (V) soccer (O).

B.   *Example:* Barbara goes to the gym (place) every day (time).

1. My friends drove to Tennessee (place) last Friday (time).
2. The teacher read the announcement in class (place) yesterday (time).
3. The students go to the library (place) at four o'clock every afternoon (time).
4. We ate at a good restaurant (place) last week (time).

C.   *Example:* Mother made sandwiches (direct) for everyone (indirect).

1. Ted gave roses (direct) to his girlfriend (indirect).
2. I got a hotel room (direct) for Linda and Susan (indirect).
3. I mailed a letter (direct) to Bob (indirect).
4. Tom did a big favor (direct) for me (indirect).

D.
1. Ted gave roses to his girlfriend.
   Ted gave his girlfriend roses.
2. I wrote a letter to Mary.
   I wrote Mary a letter.
3. I got a hotel room for them.
   I got them a hotel room.
4. The librarian read a story to the children.
   The librarian read the children a story.
5. The man bought a car for his son.
   The man bought his son a car.
6. Please do a favor for me.
   Please do me a favor.
7. Bob won't tell the truth to us.
   Bob won't tell us the truth.
8. They are going to send the pictures to you.
   They are going to send you the pictures.

Tape Script—Lesson 5

E. **Listening Comprehension**

   A man, who is an engineer in his early forties, brought his injured son to the emergency room of the hospital. The boy was severely hurt in a motorcycle accident. His mother was not home at the time and did not know about the tragedy.
   "Please save my boy," the man pleaded with the doctors. "He's my only child."
   "We'll do our best," the emergency room doctors tried to reassure him. "We have an excellent surgeon who will operate on him immediately."
   The doctors took the boy to surgery, but the surgeon gave an anguished cry. "Oh, no, not my son, my only child!"

Question: What is the relationship of the boy to the engineer and the surgeon?

F. **Dictation**

1. The medicine which the doctor gave me tastes awful.
2. The students whose papers I corrected were happy.
3. The boy tries to go to the gym twice a week for some exercise.
4. That teacher whom I know well speaks Spanish fluently.

End of lesson 5

Lesson 6: Making Comparisons

Vocabulary Focus

1. a. I see the girl walking down the street.
   b. Do you see the bird in the tree?
   c. They're going to see many interesting sights in Mexico.
   d. Let's go see the new movie playing downtown.

2. a. I'm looking at the teacher now.
   b. Mary is looking at her paper.
   c. Look at me! Look at what I can do!
   d. Please look at the example on page 50.

3. a. I watch TV every evening.
   b. The children are watching the baseball game.
   c. Can we watch you bake bread?
   d. Watch the road carefully when you drive.

4. a. Children often stare at people.
   b. Most people become embarrassed when someone stares at them.
   c. Is it polite or rude to stare at someone?

5. a. We can learn about human behavior from observing animal behavior.
   b. It is interesting to observe children when they play.
   c. Inexperienced teachers usually observe experienced teachers before they start teaching.
   d. Scientists do experiments and observe the results.

Let's Practice I—Comparison of Adjectives and Adverbs: Comparative and Superlative Degrees

A.
1. A pen is cheap. What about a pencil?
   A pencil is cheaper than a pen.
2. A hamburger tastes good. What about a steak?
   A steak tastes better than a hamburger.
3. The Amazon River is long. What about the Nile?
   The Nile is longer than the Amazon.
4. Japan is far. What about China?
   China is farther than Japan.
5. Paris is old. What about Rome?
   Rome is older than Paris.
6. A briefcase is heavy. What about a suitcase?
   A suitcase is heavier than a briefcase.
7. A sewing machine is noisy. What about a washing machine?
   A washing machine is noisier than a sewing machine.
8. Our team fought hard. What about their team?
   Their team fought harder than our team.
9. John drove fast. What about Bill?
   Bill drove faster than John.
10. Julie jumped high. What about her brother?
    Her brother jumped higher than Julie did.

B.
1. A desk chair is comfortable. What about an armchair?
   An armchair is more comfortable than a desk chair.
2. A gold ring is expensive. What about a diamond ring?
   A diamond ring is more expensive than a gold ring.
3. A television is important. What about a telephone?
   A telephone is more important than a television.
4. Animals are intelligent. What about human beings?
   Human beings are more intelligent than animals.
5. A rat is dangerous. What about a lion?
   A lion is more dangerous than a rat.
6. Rita spoke clearly. What about her sister?
   Her sister spoke more clearly than Rita did.
7. John worked patiently. What about his father?
   His father worked more patiently than John did.
8. The boy walked slowly. What about the old man?
   The old man walked more slowly than the boy did.
9. Jim writes legibly. What about Ken?
   Ken writes more legibly than Jim.
10. The boys finished early. What about the girls?
    The girls finished earlier than the boys.

C.
1. John is tall.
   He's the tallest boy in our class.
2. This restaurant is good.
   It's the best restaurant in town.
3. That restaurant is bad.
   It's the worst restaurant in town.
4. Judy is lazy.
   Judy is the laziest girl I know.
5. Mark is patient.
   He's the most patient person I know.
6. The museum is famous.
   It's one of the most famous museums in the world.
7. Bob works hard.
   He works the hardest of all.
8. Susan swam far.
   She swam the farthest of anyone else.
9. Fred spoke seriously.
   He spoke the most seriously of all.
10. Sam answered angrily.
    He answered the most angrily of all.

D.
1. Jack weighs 60 kilograms. Bert weighs 72 kilograms, and George weighs 81 kilograms. Who is the heaviest of all?
   George is the heaviest of all.
2. Linda's height is 167 centimeters. Nancy's height is 170 centimeters. Cindy's height is 160 centimeters. Who is the tallest girl?
   Nancy is the tallest girl.
3. Bill ran one mile in 9 minutes. Ted ran a mile in 10 minutes, and Carlos ran a mile in 9 and a half minutes. Who ran the fastest?
   Bill ran the fastest.

Tape Script—Lesson 6

4. Chen got a score of 550 on the TOEFL exam. Kim got a score of 570 on the TOEFL exam, and Jose got 515. Who did the best on the TOEFL exam?
   Kim did the best on the TOEFL exam.
5. Harvard University was founded in 1636. Stanford University was founded in 1891. Yale University was founded in 1701. Which one is the oldest university?
   Harvard is the oldest university.
6. Mike goes to bed at midnight every night. Henry stays up till one in the morning. Lisa goes to bed by 11:30. Who goes to bed the earliest? Who goes to bed the latest?
   Lisa goes to bed the earliest. Henry goes to bed the latest.

Let's Practice II—Expressions of Equality, Similarity, and Difference: *As, The Same As, Like,* and *Different From*

A. 1. Kathy is friendly. Dave is also friendly.
       Dave is as friendly as Kathy.
    2. Kathy is intelligent. Dave is also intelligent.
       Dave is as intelligent as Kathy.
    3. Ruth is 19 years old. Betsy is 19 years old too.
       Betsy is as old as Ruth.
    4. Ali drives carefully. Mohammed drives carefully too.
       Mohammed drives as carefully as Ali.
    5. Bob is serious. Sam is less serious.
       Sam is not as serious as Bob.
    6. Mark thinks quickly. Paul thinks less quickly.
       Paul doesn't think as quickly as Mark.
    7. Turtles are slow. Snails are slower.
       Snails are not as fast as turtles.
    8. The weather in Minneapolis is cold in the winter. The weather in New York is warmer.
       The weather in New York is not as cold as the weather in Minneapolis.

B. 1. Sam is intelligent, friendly, and polite. So is Phil. Is Phil like Sam?
       Yes, Phil is like Sam.
    2. Ming comes from Beijing and Chen comes from Shanghai. Does Chen come from the same country as Ming?
       Yes, Chen comes from the same country as Ming.
    3. Does the word *ascend* mean the same as *go up*?
       Yes, *ascend* means the same as *go up*.
    4. Paul is taking a physics course. Mary is taking a chemistry course. Is Mary taking the same course as Paul?
       No, Mary isn't taking the same course as Paul. She's taking a different course from Paul.
    5. Is American football the same as European football?
       No, American football is not the same as European football. American football is different from European football.
    6. Is an escalator like a stairway?
       Yes, an escalator is like a stairway.
    7. Is the Underground the same as the subway?
       Yes, the Underground is the same as the subway.
    8. Is North American food the same as Mexican food?
       No, North American food is not the same as Mexican food. North American food is different from Mexican food.

C. 1. Is the department store farther than the drugstore?
       Yes, the department store is farther than the drugstore.
    2. What about the restaurant?
       The restaurant is farther than the drugstore.
    3. Compare the distance of the bank and the library.
       The bank is farther than the library.
    4. Is the parking structure as far as the restaurant?
       Yes, the parking structure is as far as the restaurant.
    5. Is the cafeteria as far as the department store?
       No, the cafeteria isn't as far as the department store.
    6. Which building is the closest to you?
       The drugstore is the closest to me.
    7. Which building is the tallest?
       The parking structure is the tallest.
    8. In which building are people the most quiet?
       People are the most quiet in the library.
    9. Is a cafeteria like a restaurant?
       Yes, a cafeteria is like a restaurant.
   10. Is the post office the same as the movie theater?
       No, the post office is not the same as the movie theater.

Let's Practice III—Expressions of Quantity (Part 1): Count and Noncount Nouns

A. 1. cup
       I have a cup.
    2. sugar
       I have sugar.
    3. pencil
       I have a pencil.
    4. pencils
       I have pencils
    5. toothbrush
       I have a toothbrush.
    6. toothpaste
       I have toothpaste.
    7. comb
       I have a comb.
    8. combs
       I have combs.
    9. glass
       I have a glass.
   10. milk
       I have milk.

B. 1. cup
       I have a cup.
    2. sugar
       I have some sugar.
    3. pencil
       I have a pencil.
    4. pencils
       I have some pencils.
    5. toothbrush
       I have a toothbrush.
    6. toothpaste
       I have some toothpaste.
    7. comb
       I have a comb.
    8. combs
       I have some combs.
    9. glass
       I have a glass.
   10. milk
       I have some milk.

C. 1. cup
       I don't have a cup.
    2. sugar
       I don't have any sugar.
    3. pencil
       I don't have a pencil.
    4. pencils
       I don't have any pencils.
    5. toothbrush
       I don't have a toothbrush.
    6. toothpaste
       I don't have any toothpaste.
    7. comb
       I don't have a comb.
    8. combs
       I don't have any combs.
    9. glass
       I don't have a glass.
   10. milk
       I don't have any milk.

Tape Script—Lesson 6

D. 1. coffee
     Do you need any coffee?
     Yes. Yes, I need some.
    2. ice cream
     Do you need any ice cream?
     No. No, I don't need any.
    3. a knife
     Do you need a knife?
     No. No, I don't need one.
    4. mustard
     Do you need any mustard?
     Yes. Yes, I need some.
    5. a can opener
     Do you need a can opener?
     Yes. Yes, I need one.
    6. cigarettes
     Do you need any cigarettes?
     No. No, I don't need any.
    7. a toothbrush
     Do you need a toothbrush?
     No. No, I don't need one.
    8. toothpaste
     Do you need any toothpaste?
     Yes. Yes, I need some.

Let's Practice IV—Expressions of Quantity (Part 2): *A Lot Of, A Little, A Few, Enough, Many, and Much*

A. Example: _a little_

   1. There are many department stores downtown. _many_
   2. There are only a few people on the bus. _a few_
   3. John needs a lot of time to finish the report. _a lot of_
   4. Did you have much trouble with this assignment? _much_
   5. I don't have many good clothes. _many_
   6. My parents receive a lot of mail every day. _a lot of_
   7. Jane has only a few close friends. _a few_
   8. Linda puts a little sugar in her coffee. _a little_
   9. Do you have enough stamps for all these letters? _enough_
   10. Peter doesn't have much money left. _much_

B. 1. Tom ate a lot of potato chips. In fact . . .
     In fact, he ate too many potato chips.
    2. Mary drank a lot of beer. In fact . . .
     In fact, she drank too much beer.
    3. Bob has a lot of girlfriends. In fact . . .
     In fact, he has too many girlfriends.
    4. Mr. Jones put a lot of sugar in his coffee. In fact . . .
     In fact, he put too much sugar in his coffee.
    5. Mrs. Jones grew a lot of tomatoes in her garden. In fact . . .
     In fact, she grew too many tomatoes in her garden.
    6. Sam lent Paul a lot of money. In fact . . .
     In fact, he lent Paul too much money.

Tape Script—Lesson 6

C. **True/False**

Example: a. T (F) b. (T) F

1. Linda attends several classes and lectures four days a week; she has none on Tuesday. But she spends a few hours in the biology lab every Tuesday where she examines a lot of slides under the microscope.
   True or false: a. Linda has either classes or a lab every day.   T
   　　　　　　　 b. Linda hears a lecture in the biology lab every Tuesday.   F

2. Linda also has to do a couple of experiments every day for chemistry. She never has enough time to finish everything.
   True or false: a. Linda always has time to complete her work.   F
   　　　　　　　 b. Linda does two experiments for chemistry every day.   T

3. Linda has some bad days when she complains that there is too much pressure on her to complete all her course requirements. Still she has no regrets about choosing medicine as her career. There is no other field that interests her.
   True or false: a. Linda sometimes wishes that she had chosen another field than medicine.   F
   　　　　　　　 b. Linda enjoys her courses every day.   F

D. **Dictation**

1. Do you remember many things from your childhood?
2. For dinner I ate a lot of fish and rice, a little salad, and a few vegetables.
3. Traveling by train is not as fast as traveling by plane but it's usually more comfortable.

End of lesson 6

Lesson 7: Houses and Apartments

Conversation

At the Housing Office

Receptionist: Hello. May I help you?
Embolo: Yes, please. I'm a new student from West Africa and I need a place to live.
Receptionist: Do you prefer a room in a private house, an apartment, or a dormitory?
Embolo: Which is the cheapest?
Receptionist: Probably a room in a private house.
Embolo: I want to live on a quiet street.
Receptionist: Here is a list of available rooms. You should check in the newspaper too.
Embolo: Thank you very much.

Vocabulary Focus

Rooms of the House and Furniture

A.
1. living room
2. dining room
3. kitchen
4. family room
5. bedroom
6. bathroom
7. laundry room
8. basement
9. first floor
10. second floor
11. attic

B.
1. What furniture is in the living room?
   There's a sofa, an armchair, and a coffee table in the living room.
2. What furniture is in the dining room?
   There's a dining table and three chairs in the dining room.
3. What furniture is in the bedroom?
   There's a bed and a dresser in the bedroom.
4. What appliances are in the kitchen?
   There's a refrigerator, a sink, and a stove with an oven in the kitchen.
5. What fixtures are in the bathroom?
   There's a bathtub, a sink, and a toilet in the bathroom.

Let's Practice I—Expressions of Place: *In, At, On*

A.
1. Do the Smiths live in the city or the suburbs?
   They live in the suburbs.
2. Do they live in a house or an apartment?
   They live in a house.
3. What is their address?
   There address is 33 Walden Road.
4. Are the children playing indoors or outdoors?
   They are playing outdoors.
5. Where is the bicycle?
   It's in the garage.
6. Where is the cat lying?
   It's lying in the driveway.
7. Do you think the Smiths live on a busy or a quiet street?
   I think they live on a quiet street.
8. Where do you think Mr. and Mrs. Smith are?
   I think they are in the house.

B. 1. Do you live in a city, a town, or a village?
2. Do you live in a house or an apartment?
3. Do you live on a quiet or a busy street?
4. What street do you live on?
5. How many floors does your home have?
6. How many rooms are there in your home?

C. **Listening Comprehension**

Last year Tim was living with his uncle's family, and his friend Bill was living in the dormitory. This year both boys decided to share an apartment. They didn't have a car, so they wanted a place near the campus. They were lucky. They found a fairly large furnished apartment half a mile from the university. It was hot and humid the day they moved. They borrowed a friend's truck and worked from nine in the morning to three in the afternoon. Besides clothing, books, and school supplies, they brought several posters to hang on the walls. They also had a television set, a stereo, a window fan, and even a small computer. By the end of the day they were both tired but happy.

Questions

1. Who was Tim living with last year?
   He was living with his uncle's family last year.
2. Where was Bill living last year?
   Bill was living in the dormitory.
3. What did the two boys decide to do this year?
   They decided to share an apartment.
4. What kind of apartment did they find?
   They found a fairly large furnished apartment.
5. How far was the apartment from the university?
   It was half a mile from the university.
6. What was the weather like the day they moved?
   It was hot and humid the day they moved.
7. What were some of the things that they brought into their apartment?
   They brought clothes, books, posters, a television set, and even a computer.
8. How did the boys feel by the end of the day?
   They felt tired but happy by the end of the day.

Let's Practice II—The Definite Article: *The*

A. *Example:* 1. . . . *a* house. *The* house . . .

1. . . . *a* can . . . *The* paint . . .
2. *The* used . . . . . . *a* good . . .
3. *The* little . . . . . . *a* quarter . . . *the* street.
4. . . . *a* cake. *The* cake . . .
5. . . . *an* extra . . . *The* chair . . .
6. . . . *a* big . . . *The* fish . . .
7. *The* key . . . . . . *a* duplicate . . .
8. . . . *a* good . . . *The* movie . . . . . . *an* award.

Tape Script—Lesson 7

B. *Example:* X Captain Harkness
The old man . . . . . . *the* street.

1. X Alarm . . .
2. *The* alarm . . .
3. . . . X South America?
4. X Queen . . . . . . X other . . .
5. *The* queen . . .
6. *The* telephone . . . . . . X Alexander . . .
7. . . . X Central . . .
8. X were . . . . . . *the* park.
9. . . . X Lake . . .
10. *The* Andes . . . *the* highest
11. *The* convict . . . . . . X prison.
12. . . . X class . . . . . . *the* library.

C. 1. What is the second longest river in the world? The Amazon
  The Amazon is the second longest river in the world.
2. What is the largest desert in the world? The Sahara
  The Sahara is the largest desert in the world.
3. What is the longest river in North America? The Mississippi
  The Mississippi is the longest river in North America.
4. What is the largest ocean in the world? The Pacific
  The Pacific is the largest ocean in the world.

Let's Practice III—Comparison of Nouns: Comparative and Superlative Degrees

A. 1. Mike drinks a lot of milk. Phil drinks a little milk. Who drinks more milk?
  Mike drinks more milk than Phil.
2. Ron ate three apples. Liz ate four apples. Who ate fewer apples?
  Ron ate fewer apples than Liz.
3. Mike drinks a lot of milk. Phil drinks a little milk. Who drinks less milk?
  Phil drinks less milk than Mike.
4. Joan made ten mistakes. Jill made six mistakes. Karen made three mistakes. Who made the most mistakes?
  Joan made the most mistakes.
  Who made the fewest mistakes?
  Karen made the fewest mistakes.
5. Susan spent a hundred dollars. Sam spent fifty dollars. Jane spent ten dollars. Who spent the most money?
  Susan spent the most money.
  Who spent the least money?
  Jane spent the least money.

B. 1. Mark has two radios and so does Mary.
  Mary has as many radios as Mark.
2. Pam has three pens and so does Jerry.
  Jerry has as many pens as Pam.
3. I drank a lot of coffee for breakfast and so did you.
  You drank as much coffee for breakfast as I.
4. Ted has a lot of work to do and so does Frank.
  Frank has as much work to do as Ted.
5. You read six books last month and so did Linda.
  Linda read as many books last month as you.
6. Dan needs a lot of help and George does too.
  George needs as much help as Dan.

Tape Script—Lesson 7

Let's Practice IV—Demonstrative Adjectives and Pronouns: *This, These, That*, and *Those*

A. *Example: This* chair . . .   . . . *that* chair . . .

    1. *This* book . . .   . . . *that* one . . .
    2. *Those* pencils . . .   . . . *these* pencils . . .
    3. *These* shoes . . .   . . . *those* others . . .
    4. *This* glass . . .   . . . *that* one.
    5. *That*'s not . . .   . . . *This* is . . .
    6. *These* students . . .   . . . *those* students . . .

B. 1. I ate an apple.
     I want to eat another one.
   2. I saw a good movie.
     I want to see another one.
   3. I found a dollar bill.
     I want to find another one.
   4. I bought a good book.
     I want to buy another one.

C. 1. Some people like to swim and other people like to run.
   2. Some courses are easy and other courses are difficult.
   3. Some days are good and other days are bad.
   4. Some books are interesting and others are boring.
   5. Some people are friendly and others are not.
   6. Some jokes are funny and others are corny.

D. 1. We saw two apartments.
     What were they like? old / modern
     One was old and the other was modern.
   2. We saw six apartments.
     What were they like? cheap / expensive
     One was cheap and the others were expensive.
   3. We saw two bedrooms.
     What were they like? large / small
     One was large and the other was small.
   4. We saw two bathrooms.
     What were they like? clean / dirty
     One was clean and the other was dirty.
   5. We saw five closets.
     What were they like? roomy / tiny
     One was roomy and the others were tiny.

E. 1. For rent: two bedroom furnished
     apartment in modern building on
     quiet street. Utilities paid. $350. Call
     manager at 922-8671, Monday through
     Friday, five to eight P.M.

   2. Available for fall occupancy:
     efficiency apartments on campus.
     Unfurnished. Utilities included except
     electricity. Large room with balcony.
     $190. Call 416-4473.

Tape Script—Lesson 7

    3. Second floor: four rooms. Stove, refrigerator and drapes furnished. $400 a month plus electricity. First and last month's rent due upon occupancy. No pets, no children. Call 382-2569.

    4. Green Meadows Apartments. Now renting one and two bedroom apartments. Washer, dryer, dishwasher in each apartment. Carpeting, drapes, recreational facilities. Renting from $285. 4141 Green Meadows Boulevard. Bellevue. Phone 597-0839.

F. Dictation
1. This sweater is too large, and the other one is too small.
2. Mrs. Jones didn't spend as much money yesterday as Mrs. Smith did.
3. If you want to see beautiful scenery, the view along the California coast is superb.

End of lesson 7

Lesson 8: Making Requests and Complaints

Conversation

A. **In the Department Store**

Clerk: May I help you?
Customer: Yes, I'd like to try on these pants.
Clerk: Certainly. The fitting room is straight back.
Customer: Could I try on a shirt too?
Clerk: Go right ahead.

Now repeat the conversation after the speaker.

B. **In the Apartment**

Tenant: Something's wrong with the kitchen sink.
Landlord: What's the matter with it?
Tenant: It leaks continuously. Could you please fix it?
Landlord: Sure. I'll call the plumber.

Now repeat the conversation after the speaker.

C. **At the Complaint Department**

Customer: I have a complaint to make.
Clerk: Yes, what is it?
Customer: I bought this lamp here a week ago, but it doesn't work.
Clerk: May I see your receipt please?
Customer: Here it is.
Clerk: I'll have the electrician repair it. I'll call you in a few days when it's ready.
Customer: Thank you.

Now repeat the conversation after the speaker.

D. **In the Dormitory**

Foreign Student: Excuse me. Could you please turn down your stereo. It's too loud. I can't study or sleep.
American Student: What did you say? I can't hear you.
Foreign Student: Would you mind turning down your stereo?
American Student: What? Speak louder.
Foreign Student: Please TURN DOWN your stereo.
American Student: Sorry. Can't hear a word you're saying.
Foreign Student: TURN DOWN YOUR STEREO!
American Student: Oh, O.K. I will.

Questions

1. What did the foreign student ask the American student?
   He asked him to turn down his stereo.
2. Why did he ask him to turn down his stereo?
   Because it was too loud.
3. What did the American student say to the foreign student?
   The American student said that he couldn't hear him.
4. What did the foreign student finally do to make the American student hear him?
   He finally spoke very loud. He shouted.

Tape Script—Lesson 8

Vocabulary Focus

1. The Verb *Get*

   1. get angry
   2. get bored
   3. get hurt
   4. get drunk
   5. get nervous
   6. get embarrassed
   7. get red
   8. get rich
   9. get poor
   10. get lost
   11. get excited
   12. get cold
   13. get hot
   14. get dark
   15. get frightened
   16. get used to

   17. John got embarrassed when he made a mistake. His face and ears got red.
   18. It gets very cold in Minneapolis in the winter time.
   19. Many people want to get rich fast.
   20. Laura got nervous before her exam.

2. *Be Used To, Get Used To*

   1. Mr. Lee has lived in Toronto for twenty years. He is used to the way of life in North America.
   2. He has worked hard all his life. He is used to working hard.
   3. Mrs. Jones comes from a small town. She wasn't used to big cities, but she is getting used to them now.
   4. Jose Torres has been living in California for two years. He wasn't used to eating hot dogs and hamburgers, but he is getting used to eating them now.

Let's Practice I—Requests and Suggestions

A. 1. Please give this letter to Jane.
       Will you please give this letter to Jane?
    2. Please answer me soon.
       Will you please answer me soon?
    3. Please be on time.
       Will you please be on time?
    4. Hurry!
       Will you please hurry?
    5. Come back tomorrow.
       Will you please come back tomorrow?
    6. Sign your name.
       Will you please sign your name?

B. 1. Please give this letter to Jane.
       Could you please give this letter to Jane?
    2. Please answer me soon.
       Could you please answer me soon?
    3. Please be on time.
       Could you please be on time?
    4. Hurry!
       Could you please hurry?
    5. Sign your name.
       Could you please sign your name?

C.
1. Your friend is coming into the living room now. sit down
   Would you please sit down?
2. You ask the teacher to speak more slowly. speak
   Would you please speak more slowly?
3. You tell John to come back tomorrow. come back
   Would you please come back tomorrow?
4. Mary is going to leave soon; you need to contact her tomorrow but you don't know her phone number. give me
   Would you please give me your telephone number?
5. You are walking down the street and need to know what time it is. You don't have a watch. You see someone passing by you and you ask him for the time. tell me
   Would you please tell me what time it is?

D.
1. Won't you have a piece of cake?
   Yes, thank you.
2. Would you like another cup of coffee?
   No, thank you. I've had enough.
3. Would you please open the window?
   Certainly.
4. Will you please take a message?
   Sure.
5. Could you please mail this letter for me?
   Of course. I'd be glad to.
6. Can you give me a ride home today?
   I'm sorry but I can't. I'm not going straight home.

E.
1. Let's go shopping.
   How about going shopping?
2. Let's listen to the English tapes.
   How about listening to the English tapes?
3. Let's play football.
   How about playing football?
4. Let's watch TV.
   How about watching TV?
5. Let's go to the store.
   How about going to the store?
6. Let's have pizza tonight.
   How about having pizza tonight?

F.
1. Shall I pick you up at seven tomorrow?
   Yes, please do. That will be fine.
2. Shall we go to the movies tonight?
   Yes, let's. That will be fun.
3. Shall we have class outdoors?
   No, let's not. The weather isn't good enough.
4. Shall I give you an exam today?
   No, please don't.
5. Shall I sing a song for you?
   Sure, if you want to.
6. Shall we speak our native language in English class?
   No, that's not a very good idea.

Tape Script—Lesson 8

Let's Practice II—Adverbs of Intensification: *Very, Too, Much,* and *Enough*

A. 1. Mark was driving fast down the freeway. He was doing 80 miles an hour but the speed limit was 55.
       Mark was driving too fast.
    2. The girl was very nervous and couldn't speak.
       The girl was too nervous.
    3. Those people are very frightened. They won't get in the airplane.
       Those people are too frightened.
    4. Eric worked very slowly and didn't finish everything.
       Eric worked too slowly.
    5. Mr. Hart spoke very frankly and made people angry.
       Mr. Hart spoke too frankly.
    6. The children walked very slowly to school and arrived 15 minutes late.
       The children walked too slowly.

B. 1. Are you strong enough to carry a suitcase? Yes
       Yes, I'm strong enough to carry a suitcase.
    2. Are you strong enough to lift ten kilograms? Yes
       Yes, I'm strong enough to lift ten kilograms.
    3. Are you strong enough to lift a hundred kilograms? No
       No, I'm not strong enough to lift a hundred kilograms.
    4. Are you smart enough to learn English? Yes
       Yes, I'm smart enough to learn English.
    5. Are you small enough to crawl into a mouse hole? No
       No, I'm not small enough to crawl into a mouse hole.

C. **A Bad House**

    Clarence and Bessie Beane rented a furnished house from a very bad landlord. The house was in terrible condition, but Clarence and Bessie were too poor to afford a better place. These were some of the problems. Bessie didn't like the kitchen because it was too small and dark to work in. The oven was too dirty to use. She was too short to reach the high cupboards and the other cupboards were too small.

Questions

1. What kind of landlord did Clarence and Bessie have?
   They had a very bad landlord.
2. Why did Clarence and Bessie have to live in that terrible house?
   Because they were too poor to afford a better place.
3. Why didn't Bessie like the kitchen?
   Because it was too small and dark to work in.
4. What was wrong with the oven?
   The oven was too dirty to use.
5. What was wrong with the cupboards?
   The cupboards were too high and too small.

Tape Script—Lesson 8

D.   A Bad House Continued

Clarence was very fat and couldn't fit into the bathtub which was too short and narrow. All of the chairs in the house were very uncomfortable because they were too hard. On the other hand, the bed was too soft to sleep in comfortably. The house smelled bad, the roof leaked, and even the garage was no good. It was too small for the Beane's car.

Questions

1. Why couldn't Clarence fit into the bathtub?
   Because he was too fat.
2. Why were all the chairs uncomfortable?
   Because they were too hard.
3. Was the bed too hard to sleep in comfortably?
   No, the bed was too soft to sleep in comfortably.
4. Did the house have a bad odor?
   Yes, the house had a bad odor.
5. What was wrong with the garage?
   It was too small for the Beane's car.

Let's Practice III—Indefinite Expressions: *Someone, No One, Anyone*

A.   *Example:*   Is someone at the door?
                   No, *no one* is there.

1. Is something wrong?
   No, *nothing* is wrong.
2. Isn't there anyone who knows the answer?
   No, there's *no one* who knows the answer.
3. Is there anything good on TV tonight?
   Yes, there's *something* good on TV tonight.
4. Do you know anything about English?
   Yes, I know *something* about English.
5. Do you like anybody in this class?
   I only like Billy and Suzy. I don't like *anyone* else.
6. Can anybody help me?
   No, *nobody* can help you.

B.   1. We didn't go anywhere yesterday.
      We went nowhere yesterday.
   2. I don't know of anybody who will do it.
      I know of nobody who will do it.
   3. Mr. Jones couldn't say anything.
      Mr. Jones could say nothing.
   4. Isn't there anything you would like?
      Is there nothing you would like?
   5. She didn't go anywhere without him.
      She went nowhere without him.
   6. Doesn't anyone want to go?
      Does no one want to go?

Tape Script—Lesson 8

Let's Practice IV—Elliptical Verb Forms

A.
1. I'm listening to English now.
   I am too.
2. I went to the store last week.
   I did too.
3. I've almost finished the lesson.
   I have too.
4. I'll meet her in front of the library.
   I will too.
5. I want to leave now.
   I do too.
6. I worked hard yesterday.
   I did too.

B.
1. I'm listening to English now.
   So am I.
2. I went to the store last week.
   So did I.
3. I've almost finished the lesson.
   So have I.
4. I'll meet her in front of the library.
   So will I.
5. I want to leave now.
   So do I.
6. I worked hard yesterday.
   So did I.

C. **Dictation**

1. I haven't taken the exam yet and Tom hasn't either.
2. John didn't finish his work and neither did Mary.
3. Bob isn't going to the dance, but we are.
4. Frank's already done his homework, but I haven't.

End of lesson 8

Lesson 9: Necessity and Obligation

Conversation

Appointment Calendar

1. What should Mark do on Sunday afternoon?
   He should visit his grandfather in the hospital on Sunday afternoon.
2. What had Mark better do on Sunday night?
   Mark had better study for his chemistry test on Sunday night.
3. What three things is Mark supposed to do on Monday?
   Mark is supposed to mail a valentine to Mary Ann, drop off his suit at the dry cleaner's, and go to basketball practice at four.
4. What does Mark have to do at 11 o'clock on Tuesday?
   Mark has to go to the dentist at 11 o'clock on Tuesday.
5. How much money is Mark required to pay for his parking ticket?
   Mark is required to pay three dollars.
6. When is Mark supposed to pick up his suit at the cleaner's?
   Mark is supposed to pick up his suit at the cleaner's on Friday morning.
7. What had Mark better do on Saturday morning?
   Mark had better go to the library on Saturday morning.
8. Where is he supposed to go Saturday night?
   He is supposed to go to the dance contest Saturday night.

Vocabulary Focus

The Verb *Take*

1. take a course
   Tom is taking biology this semester.
2. take an exam
   Ali took the English exam last month.
3. take a walk
   We took a walk in the park.
4. take a trip
   Our friends are taking a trip to Europe this summer.
5. take a bus
   I'll take the bus to Chicago.
6. take a bath
   Fred always takes his bath in the morning.
7. take a break
   After playing for half an hour, the band took a break for ten minutes.
8. take time
   It takes a long time to learn another language well.
9. take pictures
   I'm planning to take a lot of pictures on my trip.
10. take care of
    We'll have to ask a neighbor to take care of our cat when we go away.

Let's Practice I—Expressions of Necessity: *Must, Have To, Be Required To*

A. 1. I have to fill up my tank with gas.
       I must fill up my tank with gas.
    2. John has to stop at a gas station too.
       John must stop at a gas station too.

Tape Script—Lesson 9

       3. Sam has to change the oil.
         Sam must change the oil.
       4. You have to check the tires.
         You must check the tires.

B.   1. They must buy a new battery tomorrow.
         They had to buy a new battery yesterday.
      2. Frank must change the flat tire this afternoon.
         Frank had to change the flat tire yesterday afternoon.
      3. We must buy a new car next week.
         We had to buy a new car last week.
      4. We must look for a used car tomorrow.
         We had to look for a used car yesterday.

C.   1. You must pay the rent on time.
         You are required to pay the rent on time.
      2. Did they have to pay a lot of bills last month?
         Were they required to pay a lot of bills last month?
      3. Do the students have to take another English course?
         Are the students required to take another English course?
      4. John must pay for his books.
         John is required to pay for his books.

D.   1. go when the light turns red
         You mustn't go when the light turns red.
      2. smoke in a No Smoking section
         You mustn't smoke in a No Smoking section.
      3. forget to say thank you
         You mustn't forget to say thank you.
      4. fight with your brother
         You mustn't fight with your brother.

E.   1. John was coughing and sneezing yesterday. He isn't in class today. sick
         He must be sick.
      2. I just went to Ann's house and rang the doorbell. She didn't answer. not home
         She must not be home.
      3. Susan just spilled coffee on her best friend. Her face became very red. embarrassed
         She must be embarrassed.
      4. Somebody just wrecked Sam's new motorcycle. How must Sam feel? angry
         He must feel angry.
      5. Jimmy is hardly eating any of his supper. not hungry
         He must not be hungry.
      6. We were expecting the train to come at noon, but it isn't here yet. late
         It must be late.

Let's Practice II—Expressions of Obligation: *Should, Ought To, Had Better,* and *Be Supposed To*

A.   1. I should call my friend tonight.
         I ought to call my friend tonight.
      2. You should come to class on time.
         You ought to come to class on time.
      3. People should eat fresh fruit daily.
         People ought to eat fresh fruit daily.
      4. Dentists say that you should brush your teeth right after eating.
         Dentists say that you ought to brush your teeth right after eating.

Tape Script—Lesson 9

B.
1. Should we eat fruits and vegetables every day?
   Yes, we should eat fruits and vegetables every day.
2. Should we get some exercise every day?
   Yes, we should get some exercise every day.
3. Should we smoke a lot of cigarettes every day?
   No, we shouldn't smoke a lot of cigarettes every day.
4. Should we drink strong coffee at night?
   No, we shouldn't drink strong coffee at night.

C.
1. Jane received a letter from her boyfriend. I expect she is happy.
   She should be happy.
2. The children go to the park often. I don't expect they will get lost.
   They shouldn't get lost.
3. Our friends are arriving this week. We're expecting them to arrive soon.
   They should be arriving soon.
4. Eric has been working hard all day. I expect he will be very tired tonight.
   He should be very tired tonight.
5. There is an exam tomorrow. I expect the students are studying for it.
   They should be studying for it.
6. John will have to do the experiment again. I don't expect he will make any mistakes this time.
   He shouldn't make any mistakes this time.

D. *Example:* should brush

1. should eat
2. shouldn't consume
3. must have
4. mustn't smoke
5. must obtain
6. shouldn't wait

Let's Practice III—Past of Modal Auxiliary Verbs (Part 1): *Must Have* and *Should Have*

A.
1. They came late. get lost
   They must have gotten lost.
2. You worked for a long time. be busy
   You must have been busy.
3. The children started a fire. be playing with matches
   They must have been playing with matches.
4. Mike has to repeat the course. not pass
   He must not have passed.
5. The little boy has a red face and tears on his cheeks. be crying
   He must have been crying.
6. The ground is wet. rain
   It must have rained.

B.
1. They should have been on time.
2. He should have been listening to the teacher.
3. It should be arriving now.
4. I shouldn't have taken it.
5. It should have come by now.
6. They shouldn't have been passing notes.

Tape Script—Lesson 9

C. 1. Joe was coughing in class yesterday. He stayed home from school today.
       He must have caught a cold.
    2. Mr. Adams drove through a red light.
       He must not have seen the red light.
    3. Lucy couldn't get up for her 8 o'clock class this morning.
       She must have been too tired.
    4. Mr. and Mrs. Beane weren't speaking to each other yesterday.
       They must have had a fight.

D. 1. Mark, a high school student, went fishing on Wednesday morning. What should he have been doing instead?
       He should have been in school.
    2. Mr. Morris said some bad things to his boss. What shouldn't he have said?
       He shouldn't have said some bad things to his boss.
    3. The teacher refused to help the students with the assignment. What shouldn't he have done?
       He shouldn't have refused to help the students with the assignment.
    4. Bob failed his French test. What should he have done last night?
       He should have studied for his test.

E. **Listening Comprehension**

   Eddie Cox was always looking for a good deal. One day a strange man named Joe came to Eddie's dry cleaning store and said that he would sell Eddie a color TV set for a hundred dollars. Eddie thought that was a good price because new color TV sets usually cost five hundred dollars or more. Joe told Eddie to give him the hundred dollars and he would bring him the TV in an hour. Eddie gave Joe one hundred dollars in cash. Joe left Eddie's store in a hurry and that was the last time anyone ever saw him. Joe never delivered the TV to Eddie and he never returned the hundred dollars to him.

   Questions

   1. What was Eddie always looking for?
      He was always looking for a good deal.
   2. When Joe told Eddie that he would sell him the TV for a hundred dollars, what must Eddie have been thinking?
      He must have been thinking that it was a good deal.
   3. What should Eddie have done when Joe asked him for the hundred dollars?
      He should have waited until Joe brought him the TV set.
   4. Why shouldn't Eddie have given Joe the hundred dollars at that time?
      Because Joe hadn't brought him the TV set yet.
   5. How did Joe leave Eddie's store?
      He left in a hurry.
   6. What must Joe have been intending to do when he entered Eddie's store?
      He must have been intending to rob Eddie.
   7. What must Eddie have done when he realized that he was robbed?
      He must have called the police.

Tape Script—Lesson 9

Let's Practice IV—*Both* and *Each, Either ... Or,* and *Neither ... Nor*

A.   *Example:*   a. F   b. T

1. Both Mr. and Mrs. Smith went to look for a new car.   a. T   b. F
2. Mr. Smith likes the two cars in the display room.   a. F   b. T
3. Both cars are equally good but each one has slightly different features.   a. T   b. F
4. George doesn't smoke cigarettes or drink alcohol.   a. T   b. F
5. Either Mary or Tom will help you.   a. F   b. F
6. Neither of the students knows the answer.   a. F   b. T

B.   Dictation

1. I should have studied harder for the exam because I didn't pass it.
2. When is Mrs. Jones supposed to call you?
3. We didn't see either the teacher or the students in the room.
4. Neither my sister nor my brother has traveled abroad.

End of lesson 9

Lesson 10: Can You Drive a Car?

Conversation

How to Drive Safely

1. Get into the car and adjust the rearview mirror.
2. Put the car in neutral and turn on the ignition.
3. Step on the clutch and shift into first gear.
4. With automatic transmission shift into drive position.
5. Step on the accelerator.
6. Use the directional signals to indicate a turn.
7. Honk your horn when it's necessary.
8. Pull up to the curb when you want to park.
9. Turn the motor off and get out of the car.
10. Keep right at all times except to pass.

Vocabulary Focus

Parts of the Car

Exterior:
1. body
2. trunk
3. windshield
4. headlights
5. parking lights
6. hood
7. tires
8. exhaust pipe
9. fender
10. bumper

Interior:
11. steering wheel
12. front seat
13. back seat
14. rearview mirror

Let's Practice I—Expressions of Ability: *Can, Could*, and *Be Able*

A.
1. I can swim.
   I'm able to swim.
2. John can ride a horse.
   John is able to ride a horse.
3. My friends couldn't find a good apartment.
   My friends weren't able to find a good apartment.
4. Can you speak Spanish?
   Are you able to speak Spanish?
5. Can George come tonight?
   Is George able to come tonight?
6. We couldn't meet them at the airport.
   We weren't able to meet them at the airport.
7. Bob could read Arabic.
   Bob was able to read Arabic.
8. I can't see you until tomorrow.
   I'm not able to see you until tomorrow.
9. Could they find your house?
   Were they able to find your house?
10. Mr. Scott couldn't take his vacation in June.
    Mr. Scott wasn't able to take his vacation in June.

B. Listening-Writing Response

1. Are you able to cook?
   Yes, I'm able to cook. (or: No, I'm not able to cook.)
2. Can you ride a horse?
   Yes, I can ride a horse. (or: No, I can't ride a horse.)
3. Is your father able to drive a car?
   Yes, my father is able to drive a car. (or: No, my father isn't able to drive a car.)
4. Is your mother able to drive a car?
   Yes, my mother is able to drive a car. (or: No, my mother isn't able to drive a car.)
5. Could you run fast when you were young?
   Yes, I could run fast when I was young. (or: No, I couldn't run fast when I was young.)
6. Are you able to understand these questions?
   Yes, I'm able to understand these questions. (or: No, I'm not able to understand these questions.)

C. Listening Comprehension

1. Frank wasn't able to pay for his meal.
   Why not?
   He lost his wallet.
   Oh, that's too bad.

   Question: Why couldn't Frank pay for his meal?
   Because he lost his wallet.

2. Larry was able to pass the exam.
   How?
   By studying hard.
   Oh, that's great!

   Question: How was Larry able to pass the exam?
   By studying hard.

3. Mrs. Jones was able to leave early.
   How?
   By finishing all her work.
   Oh, that's great!

   Question: How could Mrs. Jones leave early?
   By finishing all her work.

Let's Practice II—Expressions of Permission: *May, Can, Allow, Let,* and *Be Allowed To*

A.
1. I / leave class early today
   May I leave class early today?
2. We / see you in your office
   May we see you in your office?
3. We / smoke in class
   May we smoke in class?
4. I / be excused early today
   May I be excused early today?
5. I / get a drink of water
   May I get a drink of water?
6. We / have permission to do this
   May we have permission to do this?

Tape Script—Lesson 10

B. Listening-Writing Response

1. Can I go through a red light when there is no traffic?
   No, you're not allowed to.
2. Can I pay with a check in a restaurant?
   No, you can't. The management won't let you.
3. Can we eat potato chips with our fingers?
   Yes, certainly you can.
4. Can we eat rice with our fingers?
   No, you're not supposed to.
5. Can we have pets in this apartment?
   No, the landlord doesn't permit them.
6. May I sleep during class?
   No, you may not.

C. Listening-Writing Response

1. What are you supposed to do in the morning?
   I'm supposed to . . .
2. What weren't you allowed to do when you were a child?
   I wasn't allowed to . . . when I was a child.
3. What kind of visa is a foreign student required to have?
   A foreign student is required to have a special student visa.
4. Will your teacher let you smoke in English class?
   No, my teacher won't let me smoke in English class.

D. True or False?

1. The patient must have radiation treatment too.
   The patient was required to undergo radiation treatment too.   T
2. The patient shouldn't eat or drink twelve hours prior to the operation.
   The patient was supposed to eat something right before his operation.   F
3. The cost of the operation should be covered by the patient's health insurance plan.
   The health insurance company is supposed to pay for the patient's operation.   T
4. The patient has to pay extra for a private room.
   The patient isn't required to pay extra for a private room.   F
5. The patient was given sick leave from work.
   The patient was allowed to have time off from work.   T
6. Visitors may come to see patients in the afternoon or evening.
   Visitors are not allowed to see patients in the morning.   T

E.
1. No U-turn
2. No Bicycles Allowed
3. Merge Left
4. Halt!
5. Steep Grade (or Hill)
6. Lane Narrows
7. You May Not Come In
8. Pedestrian Crossing
9. Stop Light Ahead
10. Construction Equipment
11. You May Not Turn Left
12. Deer Crossing
13. Trucks Are Not Allowed on This Road
14. Bicycle Crossing
15. Divided Highway Ends
16. School Crossing
17. Two-Way Traffic
18. You Must Keep Right
19. Slippery When Wet
20. You Must Let the Other Car Go First

Tape Script—Lesson 10

Let's Practice III—Making Questions by Rising Intonation

A. 1. Mr. Jones broke his leg?
 Yes, he did.
 2. You're not finished yet?
 No, I'm not.
 3. Mary lost her wallet?
 Yes, unfortunately.
 4. The students haven't registered yet?
 No, not yet.

B. 1. Jeffrey won the race.
 Jeffrey won the race?
 2. It snowed last night.
 It snowed last night?
 3. You were late.
 You were late?
 4. They haven't started the book yet.
 They haven't started the book yet?
 5. Fred and Emily got married.
 Fred and Emily got married?
 6. You didn't know the answer.
 You didn't know the answer?

C. 1. Ted's brother was fired yesterday.
 He was?
 2. I haven't registered for my English class yet.
 You haven't?
 3. We can't take computer science until next semester.
 We can't?
 4. My friends are moving to Japan.
 They are?
 5. Mike's found your keys.
 He has?
 6. I'm not allowed to go there alone.
 You're not?

Let's Practice IV—Tag Questions

A. 1. Mary isn't tired, is she?
 2. The doctor wasn't in her office, was she?
 3. I didn't get here too early, did I?
 4. They won't arrive until tomorrow, will they?
 5. You haven't called them yet, have you?

B. 1. Mary isn't happy, is she?
 2. You don't like that, do you?
 3. You haven't been studying, have you?
 4. We shouldn't tell lies, should we?
 5. The weather doesn't look good today, does it?

C. 1. Mary is tired, isn't she?
 2. The doctor was in her office, wasn't she?
 3. I got here too early, didn't I?
 4. They'll arrive tomorrow, won't they?
 5. You've called them already, haven't you?

D. 1. Mary is happy, isn't she?
 2. You like that, don't you?
 3. You've been studying, haven't you?
 4. We should tell the truth, shouldn't we?
 5. The weather looks good today, doesn't it?

Tape Script—Lesson 10

E.
1. He isn't here, is he?
2. You'll do it, won't you?
3. He borrowed some money from you, didn't he?
4. He hasn't forgotten, has he?
5. You've finished, haven't you?
6. You can swim, can't you?
7. He's interesting, isn't he?
8. You're ready, aren't you?
9. He doesn't know, does he?
10. You'll say it, won't you?
11. He can do it, can't he?
12. He's handsome, isn't he?
13. You've done that, haven't you?
14. He isn't telling us, is he?

F.
1. The boy doesn't know how to swim.
   The boy doesn't know how to swim, does he?
2. Bob's a careful driver.
   Bob's a careful driver, isn't he?
3. You haven't started it yet.
   You haven't started it yet, have you?
4. We can go downtown by bus.
   We can go downtown by bus, can't we?
5. Large cities are noisy.
   Large cities are noisy, aren't they?
6. Paris is a beautiful city.
   Paris is a beautiful city, isn't it?
7. They'll be happy there.
   They'll be happy there, won't they?
8. The little girl isn't afraid.
   The little girl isn't afraid, is she?

G. **Dictation**

1. Jack had better go on a diet because he's getting too fat.
2. I should have finished all my work, but I didn't.
3. The students are not allowed to smoke in class, but they may smoke in the lounge.
4. We're happy because we've been able to understand this lesson.

End of lesson 10

Lesson 11: Looking for a Job

Conversation

A. **Help Wanted**

Alex: I'm looking for a job. Where can I find one?
Mike: Look in the Classified section of the newspaper, under Help Wanted. People who need services advertise there.
Alex: Thanks. I'll try that.

B. **I need a job.**

Student: I need to find a part-time job to help support myself through school.
Counselor: How fast can you type?
Student: About sixty words a minute.
Counselor: Go to the Personnel Office and check to see if there are any part-time clerical openings.
Student: Thank you very much.

C. **I can sell anything.**

Mr. Kirby: What previous experience in sales have you had?
Fred: I started out as a clerk in the automotive department at Sears. After that I managed a used car lot for several years.
Mr. Kirby: What do you know about vacuum cleaners?
Fred: Not much, but I know I could sell them. I can sell anything.
Mr. Kirby: I'll hire you. I like your self-confidence.

D. **You're fired!**

Manager: Clayton, you're fired!
Clayton: What did I do this time, boss?
Manager: What did you do? Why, you put the wrong suits on the sale rack. We're trying to get rid of our *old* stock, not the new. We've lost hundreds of dollars in just two hours. How could you have done such a thing?
Clayton: Well sir, the customers were thrilled to see these new Italian suits at half the regular price. When the customers are happy, then I'm happy.
Manager: Well, I'm not happy, Clayton. Get out right now!

Vocabulary Focus

Occupations

Nouns
1. job
2. livelihood
3. career
4. profession
5. vocation
6. trade

Verbs
7. look for a job
8. apply for a job
9. get a job
10. resign from a job
11. hire someone
12. employ someone
13. fire someone

Let's Practice I—Expressions of Possibility: *May, Might, Can, Could,* and *It's Possible That*

A. 1. Maybe I will buy a new car.
   I may buy a new car.

137

Tape Script—Lesson 11

    2. Maybe John will get here tonight.
       John may get here tonight.
    3. Maybe Tom won't come here this summer.
       Tom may not come here this summer.
    4. Maybe Mike will be able to find a job in Louisiana.
       Mike may be able to find a job in Louisiana.

B.   1. Maybe they won't finish on time.
       They might not finish on time.
    2. Maybe Bob will get a better job some day.
       Bob might get a better job some day.
    3. Maybe she won't like me.
       She might not like me.
    4. Maybe there won't be enough information for us.
       There might not be enough information for us.

C.   1. What can we do tonight? visit your friends
       You can visit your friends tonight.
    2. When can Pedro go back to Mexico? next August
       Pedro can go back to Mexico next August.
    3. When can Mary see you? any time
       Mary can see me any time.
    4. Where could I look for a job? in the classified section of the newspaper
       You could look for a job in the classified section of the newspaper.
    5. Where could I cash a check? at the bank
       You could cash a check at the bank.
    6. How could I find out what I got on the test? ask the teacher
       You could ask the teacher.

D.   1. It is possible that they know our secret.
       They could know our secret.
    2. It's possible that they will come tomorrow.
       They could come tomorrow.
    3. It's possible that my friend will call me tonight.
       My friend could call me tonight.

E.   1. It is possible that the information is wrong.
       The information might be wrong.
    2. It is possible that we won't finish on time.
       We might not finish on time.
    3. It is possible that I won't be home later.
       I might not be home later.

Let's Practice II—Past of Modal Auxiliary Verbs (Part 2): *May Have, Might Have,* and *Could Have*

A.   1. Why didn't Jeffrey do what I told him to?
       He might not have been listening.
    2. I called up my friend but he didn't answer. He was supposed to be at home.
       He might have been taking a nap.
    3. Bob was absent from school yesterday.
       He may have been sick.
    4. Why did Mary say that? I don't believe her.
       She might not have been telling the truth.
    5. Frank was sitting next to Jill during the test and kept looking at her paper.
       Frank may have been copying Jill's answers.
    6. I went to meet Jack at the train station at 9 o'clock but he wasn't there.
       He might have missed his train.

B. Listening-Writing Response

1. How could you have lost that game? You had such a good team.
   We could have won easily, but the other team surprised us.
2. What happened to Alice? She doesn't live here anymore.
   She could have moved back to California.
3. Ruth looked very unhappy when she got her test back. Why?
   She could have failed the test.
4. Mr. Morris was supposed to pick up his wife at the airport at 4 P.M. He still wasn't there by 5 o'clock and Mrs. Morris began to worry. What could have happened?
   Mr. Morris *could have had* an accident on the road.

C. Listening Comprehension

1. I could have bought a Mercedes, but it was too expensive.
   a. You bought a Mercedes.
   (b.) You didn't buy a Mercedes.
2. I might not have noticed the bump in the road, but Jenny pointed it out before it was too late.
   (a.) You saw the bump before it was too late.
   b. You didn't see the bump before it was too late.
3. Those two students could have cheated on the test. All their answers are the same.
   a. The students didn't cheat on the test.
   (b.) It's possible that one student copied the other student's paper.
4. Leslie may have finished all her work.
   a. Leslie finished all her work already.
   (b.) We don't know if Leslie finished all her work.
5. That couldn't have been George at the door. He's in India.
   (a.) You don't believe that George was at the door.
   (b.) You think someone else was at the door.
6. Jerry might have left his wallet in his room.
   (a.) Jerry doesn't have his wallet with him now.
   (b.) Jerry could have forgotten to put his wallet in his pocket.
7. I could have called Jan yesterday, but I thought she was busy.
   (a.) You didn't call Jan yesterday.
   b. You called Jan yesterday.
8. I may have met her a long time ago.
   (a.) You don't remember meeting her.
   (b.) It's possible that you met her a long time ago.

Let's Practice III—Past Perfect Tense and Future Perfect Tense

A. 1. They've found a job, haven't they?
       They had found a job, hadn't they?
    2. Mr. Smith hasn't left town, has he?
       Mr. Smith hadn't left town, had he?
    3. You've been on vacation, haven't you?
       You had been on vacation, hadn't you?
    4. The secretary has quit her job, hasn't she?
       The secretary had quit her job, hadn't she?
    5. Mark has been working for you since Wednesday, hasn't he?
       Mark had been working for you since Wednesday, hadn't he?

B. 1. What are you studying?
       I'm studying English.
       How long had you studied English before you came to this school?
       I had studied English for two years before I came to this school.

Tape Script—Lesson 11

    2. Did you sleep well last night?
       Yes, I did.
       How long had you been sleeping when your alarm clock rang this morning?
       I had been sleeping for eight hours when my alarm clock rang this morning.

    3. Does David still smoke?
       No, he gave it up.
       How long had he smoked before he gave it up?
       He had smoked for fifteen years before he gave it up.

C. 1. Do you think you will have learned everything about English by the end of this course? No
       No, I don't think I will have learned everything about English by the end of this course.
    2. Jack and Connie are going to celebrate their wedding anniversary next June. How long will they have been married? ten years
       They will have been married ten years by next June.
    3. Mark has just started to study for his final exam tomorrow. Do you think he will have reviewed enough by tomorrow to pass the course? No
       No, I don't think he will have reviewed enough by tomorrow to pass the course.
    4. I will leave early tomorrow before you get up. Do you think I will have reached the Mexican border by the time you get up? Yes
       Yes, I think you will have reached the Mexican border by the time I get up.
    5. Will Jack have already left by the time we get back? Yes, he might.
       Yes, he might have already left by the time we get back.
    6. Do you think all wars will have ended by the next century? No
       No, I don't think all wars will have ended by the next century.

Let's Practice IV—Subordinating Conjunctions: *Before* and *After*

A. 1. I brush my hair. Then I comb it.
       I brush my hair before I comb it.
    2. I get dressed. Then I eat breakfast.
       I get dressed before I eat breakfast.
    3. I turn off the light. Then I leave the room.
       I turn off the light before I leave the room.
    4. I see my friends. Then I go to class.
       I see my friends before I go to class.
    5. I come home. Then I do my homework.
       I come home before I do my homework.
    6. I read the newspaper. Then I eat supper.
       I read the newspaper before I eat supper.

B. 1. I brush my hair. Then I comb it.
       I comb my hair after I brush it.
    2. I get dressed. Then I eat breakfast.
       I eat breakfast after I get dressed.
    3. I turn off the light. Then I leave the room.
       I leave the room after I turn off the light.
    4. I see my friends. Then I go to class.
       I go to class after I see my friends.

Tape Script—Lesson 11

C. **Listening Comprehension**

1. Mr. Scott read the newspaper after he wrote a letter.
    a. Mr. Scott read the newspaper first. Then he wrote a letter.
    (b.) Mr. Scott wrote a letter first. Then he read the newspaper.
2. Before the teacher passed out the test, she read the directions to the students.
    a. First the teacher passed out the test. Then she read the directions.
    (b.) First the teacher read the directions. Then she passed out the test.
3. After finding a parking place, Ellie got out of her car.
    (a.) Ellie got out of her car after she had found a place to park.
    b. Before she had found a place to park, Ellie got out of her car.
4. Sam played tennis first. Then he played basketball.
    (a.) Sam played basketball after he played tennis.
    b. Sam played tennis after he played basketball.
5. The little boy fell down and then started crying.
    a. Before the little boy fell down, he started crying.
    (b.) Before the little boy started crying, he fell down.
6. Frank met Tom before he met Phil.
    (a.) Frank met Phil after he met Tom.
    b. After Frank met Phil, he met Tom.
7. After Mary said good-bye, she got in her car.
    a. Mary got into her car and then said good-bye.
    (b.) Before Mary got into her car, she said good-bye.
8. Jane saw her mother and went upstairs.
    (a.) Jane saw her mother before she went upstairs.
    b. Jane saw her mother after she went upstairs.

D. **Dictation**

1. Mary was very excited yesterday after winning the race.
2. Airline passengers have to fasten their seatbelts before taking off.
3. Whenever you don't understand the teacher, what do you say?
4. Bob might have forgotten to put his wallet in his pocket.

End of lesson 11

Lesson 12: On the Road

Conversation

A. Making Travel Plans

Pierre: I still haven't been to Niagara Falls yet.
Bill: Let's go there next week. My parents' best friends live in Buffalo. They said we could visit them anytime on the way.
Pierre: We'll need a good map of the eastern United States and Canada. They say you have the best view of the Falls from the Canadian side.
Bill: If you're a member of the Triple A, you can have them chart a route for you.
Pierre: It's rather expensive to join, isn't it?
Bill: It costs $25.00 a year in this state, but they have several services, including free road repair and towing.
Pierre: Don't you think it would be more fun if we planned our own itinerary? We could study the map together and decide on a scenic route.
Bill: Yes, we should be able to take care of everything ourselves.
Pierre: That reminds me. Did I ever tell you about the time I was traveling alone at night and had a flat tire?

B. Returning Home

Pierre: I'm broke. I don't have any more money.
Bill: Me either. It looks as if we'll have to return home a week early.
Pierre: We should have brought more money with us.
Bill: We could have spent less if we had taken a tent and sleeping bags and slept at a campsite. I didn't realize how expensive motels were these days.

Vocabulary Focus

1. Indefinite *You, They,* and *One*

    1. You use a pen to write with.
    2. You use a notebook to take notes in.
    3. They make good fried chicken in that restaurant.
    4. They speak Spanish in Mexico.
    5. One does not eat soup with a fork.
    6. One should always have good manners in public.

2. The Verbs *Make* and *Do*

    Make

    A.
    1. make an appointment
    2. make a reservation
    3. make a list
    4. make a living
    5. make a promise
    6. make a deal
    7. make breakfast
    8. make the bed
    9. make a stop
    10. make the train
    11. make progress
    12. make certain
    13. make a telephone call
    14. make a request
    15. make a mistake
    16. make a discovery
    17. make a complaint
    18. make an excuse
    19. make a difference
    20. make things better

Do

1. do a favor
2. do a good job
3. do one's best
4. do good
5. do business
6. do work
7. do a problem
8. do a duty
9. do exercises
10. do research
11. do housework
12. do the shopping

B. 1. Have you (made) done an appointment to see the dentist yet?

2. What kinds of favors does your best friend make (do) for you?

3. What kind of research are the chemistry students making (doing)?

4. Did Julie (make) do a good impression on her boss?

5. The large oil companies (make) do a lot of money.

6. Are you (making) doing progress in English?

7. When do you prefer to make (do) your shopping?

8. Have you ever (made) done a complaint to your landlord?

9. The airline company made (did) business with the government.

10. When are you going to make (do) your homework?

Let's Practice I—Conditional Clauses with *If* (Part 1): Present

A. 1. I may be sick tomorrow. Then I won't go to work.
    If I am sick tomorrow, I won't go to work.
2. My alarm clock may not ring. Then I'll be late for school.
    If my alarm clock doesn't ring, I'll be late for school.
3. John may arrive tomorrow. In that case we'll meet him at the airport.
    If John arrives tomorrow, we'll meet him at the airport.
4. There may be a good program on TV. In that case I'll watch it.
    If there is a good program on TV, I'll watch it.

B. 1. What will happen if you forget your book? borrow my friend's
    If I forget my book, I'll borrow my friend's.
2. What will happen if it's very cold tomorrow? wear my coat
    If it's very cold tomorrow, I'll wear my coat.
3. What will happen if you use up all your money? be flat broke
    If I use up all my money, I'll be flat broke.
4. What will happen if you finish early? have time for a drink
    If I finish early, I'll have time for a drink.

C. 1. I won't go to class tomorrow if *(I'm not feeling well)*.
2. I don't usually watch TV if *(I have too much work to do)*.
3. I'll go to bed early tonight if *(I finish all my homework)*.
4. I always carry an umbrella if *(it is raining)*.

Tape Script—Lesson 12

D.
1. If I spend all my money, I'll be flat broke.
   If I spent all my money, I would be flat broke.
2. We won't go to school if we get sick.
   We wouldn't go to school if we got sick.
3. You won't miss the train if you hurry.
   You wouldn't miss the train if you hurried.
4. If Mary eats something, she'll feel better.
   If Mary ate something, she'd feel better.
5. They'll send us a postcard if they go to Europe.
   They'd send us a postcard if they went to Europe.
6. If I don't have to work today, I'll go to the beach with you.
   If I didn't have to work today, I'd go to the beach with you.

E.
1. What would happen if it rained on the day of our class picnic?
   Well, we'd have to have it another time.
2. What would happen if you didn't pass the course?
   I'd take it again next term.
3. What would happen if the teacher gave us a test today?
   I certainly wouldn't like it.

F.
1. If you try, you can learn how to drive.
   If you tried, you could learn how to drive.
2. Bob can see me if he comes before noon.
   Bob could see me if he came before noon.
3. We can travel to Europe if we save enough money.
   We could travel to Europe if we saved enough money.
4. If there is enough time, we can visit our friends.
   If there were enough time, we could visit our friends.

G.
1. If they can find a job, they'll be very happy.
   If they could find a job, they would be very happy.
2. John will visit us if he can.
   John would visit us if he could.
3. I'll meet you later if I can.
   I'd meet you later if I could.
4. If John can help us, we'll be grateful.
   If John could help us, we'd be grateful.

Let's Practice II—Conditional Clauses with *Unless* and Conditional Clauses with *If* (Part 2): Past

A.
1. We'll have the picnic tomorrow if it doesn't rain.
   We'll have the picnic tomorrow unless it rains.
2. If you don't help me, I can't do this problem.
   Unless you help me, I can't do this problem.
3. Mary will have to move if she doesn't find a job here.
   Mary will have to move unless she finds a job here.
4. If we have enough money, we'll buy a new car.
   Unless we don't have enough money, we'll buy a new car.

B.
1. I wouldn't go on vacation if I didn't have enough money.
   I wouldn't go on vacation unless I had enough money.
2. If you had time, you could spend the whole day at the beach.
   Unless you didn't have time, you could spend the whole day at the beach.
3. If Susan didn't love Bob, she wouldn't marry him.
   Unless Susan loved Bob, she wouldn't marry him.
4. I wouldn't stop by if it weren't convenient.
   I wouldn't stop by unless it were convenient.

C.
1. If we went to New York, we would see some of the highest buildings in the world.
   If we had gone to New York, we would have seen some of the highest buildings in the world.
2. If you traveled with a friend, you wouldn't get lonely.
   If you had traveled with a friend, you wouldn't have gotten lonely.
3. We could take a trip to Mexico if we didn't go to summer school.
   We could have taken a trip to Mexico if we hadn't gone to summer school.
4. Mary would go to the beach if she visited Hawaii.
   Mary would have gone to the beach if she had visited Hawaii.

D.
1. If Jane hadn't found a better job, would she have quit this one? No
   No, if Jane hadn't found a better job, she wouldn't have quit this one.
2. Would our team have lost all its games if it had practiced more? No
   No, our team wouldn't have lost all its games if it had practiced more.
3. If the prisoners could have escaped, would they have? Yes
   Yes, if the prisoners could have escaped, they would have.
4. Could your friends have lost weight faster if they had exercised daily? Yes, probably
   Yes, my friends probably could have lost weight faster if they had exercised daily.

E.
1. Would you have traveled around the world last year if you had been rich? *(Answer a is correct.)*
2. Mary wouldn't have bet so much money if she had thought she would lose. *(Answer b is correct.)*
3. The boy would have recovered faster if he hadn't walked so soon on his broken ankle. *(Answer b is correct.)*
4. If you had learned English well when you were young, how would that have changed your life today? *(Answer a is correct.)*

Let's Practice III—Reported Speech and Indirect Questions

A.
1. Amy says, "I'm going to win the game."
   Amy says she's going to win the game.
2. Charles says, "I must buy a new car."
   Charles says he must buy a new car.
3. Mark says, "I know all the answers on the test."
   Mark says he knows all the answers on the test.
4. The children are telling their parents, "We want to go to the zoo."
   The children are telling their parents they want to go to the zoo.

B.
1. Amy said, "I'm going to win the game."
   Amy said she was going to win the game.
2. Charles said, "I must buy a new car."
   Charles said he had to buy a new car.
3. Mark said, "I know all the answers on the test."
   Mark said he knew all the answers on the test.
4. The children were telling their parents, "We want to go to the zoo."
   The children were telling their parents they wanted to go to the zoo.

C.
1. They know we are taking the train.
   They knew we were taking the train.
2. We have heard that your sister is getting married.
   We had heard that your sister was getting married.
3. I understand that you don't like cold weather.
   I understood that you didn't like cold weather.

Tape Script—Lesson 12

    4. I think Cindy likes baseball better than basketball.
       I thought Cindy liked baseball better than basketball.
    5. Dr. Malone says he may take a trip to Alaska.
       Dr. Malone said he might take a trip to Alaska.
    6. I have heard that the price of fuel will be higher next month.
       I had heard that the price of fuel would be higher next month.
    7. John says he can come to my party.
       John said he could come to my party.
    8. The students hope they will learn English as quickly as possible.
       The students hoped they would learn English as quickly as possible.

D.   1. Which car cost the most? Do you remember?
       Do you remember which car cost the most?
    2. What time is it? Do you know?
       Do you know what time it is?
    3. Who will go with you? Have you decided?
       Have you decided who will go with you?
    4. When is your exam? Did you ask?
       Did you ask when your exam is?
    5. Where did everyone go? Do you know?
       Do you know where everyone went?
    6. Why did they eat that? Did you find out?
       Did you find out why they ate that?

E.   1. Who came early?
       I don't know who came early.
    2. What did she say?
       I don't know what she said.
    3. What time will the train come?
       I don't know what time the train will come.
    4. What did they want?
       I don't know what they wanted.

F.   **Travel Arrangements**

      Mr. and Mrs. Porter decided to go on a Caribbean cruise for two weeks during the Christmas holidays. Mrs. Porter called Regency Travel Service to find out some information about a tour for her husband and herself. The travel agent asked what weeks she wanted to go. She replied that she would like to take a two-week cruise from December 20 to January 4.

Questions

1. What did Mr. and Mrs. Porter decide to do during the Christmas holidays?
    They decided to go on a Caribbean cruise.
2. What did Mrs. Porter do to find out some information about a tour?
    Mrs. Porter called Regency Travel Service.
3. What did the travel agent ask her?
    She asked her what weeks she wanted to go.
4. What did Mrs. Porter reply?
    She replied that she would like to take a two-week cruise from December 20 to January 4.

Tape Script—Lesson 12

Let's Practice IV—Possessive Nouns

A. 1. Whose book is this? Ted
       It's Ted's book.
    2. Whose bicycle is this? Louis
       It's Louis's bicycle.
    3. Whose house is this? Mr. and Mrs. Jones
       It's Mr. and Mrs. Jones's house.
    4. Whose pencil is this? the girl
       It's the girl's pencil.
    5. Whose club is this? the girls
       It's the girls' club.
    6. Whose collar is this? the dog
       It's the dog's collar.

B. 1. The city's mayor recently attended a convention.
       The mayor of the city recently attended a convention.
    2. The Third World's population is increasing.
       The population of the Third World is increasing.
    3. China's history is fascinating.
       The history of China is fascinating.
    4. The world's economy is facing serious problems.
       The economy of the world is facing serious problems.
    5. Today's news is not good.
       The news of today is not good.
    6. One day's pay is twenty-five dollars.
       The pay of one day is twenty-five dollars.

C. **Dictation**

    1. Mr. Davis's daughter took a week's vacation in the Caribbean.
    2. What did he say the name of his street was?

End of lesson 12

Lesson 13: Writing a Letter

Conversation

A. **A Letter of Application**

Ali: Could you do me a favor, Ben?
Ben: Sure, Ali. What is it?
Ali: I need some help writing a letter of application.
Ben: Where do you want to apply?
Ali: I want to study engineering at the University of Michigan. I want to enroll in the Master's degree program.
Ben: Wow! That's a tough school to get into.
Ali: I know. You have to have good grades and get a high score on the English exam, but I think I can do it.

B. **A While Later**

Ben: Here you are, Ali. I've finished correcting your letter. There weren't many mistakes.
Ali: Thanks a million, Ben.

Vocabulary Focus

The Verbs *Say*, *Tell*, *Speak*, and *Talk*

1. tell
2. talk   tell
3. tell   said
4. said   tell
5. talked   spoke   said

Let's Practice I—Verbals: Infinitives

A. 1. It's expensive to travel to Europe.
    To travel to Europe is expensive.
 2. It's necessary to take the bus to school.
    To take the bus to school is necessary.
 3. It's enjoyable to ride a bicycle.
    To ride a bicycle is enjoyable.
 4. It isn't fun to get sick.
    To get sick isn't fun.
 5. It isn't legal to drive without a driver's license.
    To drive without a driver's license isn't legal.
 6. It isn't hard to fly a kite.
    To fly a kite isn't hard.

B. 1. What is easy for you to do? drive a car
    It's easy for me to drive a car.
 2. What is difficult for you to do? speak English all day long
    It's difficult for me to speak English all day long.
 3. What would be dangerous for you to do? walk in a busy street
    It would be dangerous for me to walk in a busy street.
 4. What would be fun for you to do? go to the beach
    It would be fun for me to go to the beach.

C. 1. When do you intend to go fishing?
   I think I'll go next Tuesday. You want to come with me?
   Yes, that would be fun.
   I can't wait to try out my new fishing rod.

   Questions: When does the boy intend to go fishing?
   He intends to go fishing next Tuesday.
   What does the boy want to try out?
   He wants to try out his new fishing rod.

2. Did you remember to buy flowers for Mother's birthday?
   Oh no, I forgot to. Now what'll we do?
   Well, let's plan to take her out for dinner. She'll like that.
   Yes, that's a good idea.

   Questions: What did the boy forget to do?
   He forgot to buy flowers for his mother's birthday.
   What did the boy and girl decide to do for their mother?
   They decided to take her out for dinner.

D. 1. Julie failed her Spanish exam. What was she ashamed to do? tell her parents
   She was ashamed to tell her parents.
2. We've made plans already for Saturday night. What won't we be able to do? go to the Smith's house
   We won't be able to go to the Smith's house.
3. The students spent many hours in the chemistry lab. What wasn't it easy to do? complete the experiments
   It wasn't easy to complete the experiments.
4. Eric won the marathon. What was he proud to do? place first in the marathon
   He was proud to place first in the marathon.

E. 1. Alice likes to have people visit her.
   Guests are welcome to visit her.   T
2. John made a lot of mistakes on his test.
   He was careful to give the correct answers.   F
3. Mary can't wait to learn to fly a plane.
   Mary is eager to fly a plane.   T
4. The teacher was willing to spend some extra time with the students.
   The teacher was reluctant to help the students.   F
5. We received good news from our parents.
   We were upset to hear from our parents.   F
6. Jenny loves mathematics.
   She's likely to become an engineer when she grows up.   T

Let's Practice II—Gerunds

A. 1. To learn chess isn't easy.
   Learning chess isn't easy.
2. To buy a brand new car is expensive.
   Buying a brand new car is expensive.
3. To win the game is important for her.
   Winning the game is important for her.
4. To make a million dollars is Mark's ambition.
   Making a million dollars is Mark's ambition.
5. To clean house all day is boring.
   Cleaning house all day is boring.
6. To forget to lock the door is foolish.
   Forgetting to lock the door is foolish.

Tape Script—Lesson 13

B. 1. working
2. reading
3. winning
4. being
5. observing
6. inviting

C. 1. Mike hates working here.
Mike hates to work here.
2. Has it started raining yet?
Has it started to rain yet?
3. I tried to reach you by phone.
I tried reaching you by phone.
4. Judy prefers to walk to school.
Judy prefers walking to school.
5. When did Michelle begin to study English?
When did Michelle begin studying English?
6. Did your friend ever try getting his money back?
Did your friend ever try to get his money back?

D. 1. My father put the newspaper down and asked me a question.
What did my father stop doing? reading the newspaper
Your father stopped reading the newspaper.
What did my father stop to do? ask a question
Your father stopped to ask a question.

2. I remembered something. I left the car keys on the table.
What did I remember doing? leaving the car keys on the table
You remembered leaving the car keys on the table.

3. Jane told Bob to call her at nine.
What will Bob remember to do? call Jane at nine
Bob will remember to call Jane at nine.

4. I didn't forget to lock the door.
What did I remember to do? lock the door
You remembered to lock the door.

5. I was watching TV. Then the phone rang.
What did I stop doing? watching TV
You stopped watching TV.
What did I stop to do? answer the phone
You stopped to answer the phone.

Let's Practice III—Verbs That Take a Noun Followed by the Infinitive and Verbs and Adjectives of Desire, Necessity, and Urgency Followed by a Noun Clause

A. 1. What did your mother remind you to do?
My mother reminded me to say "please" and "thank you."
2. What did Jack's father convince Jack to do?
He convinced him to save his money for college.
3. What did Mrs. Clark invite you to do?
She invited me to come to dinner next Saturday.
4. What do parents expect their children to do?
Parents expect their children to be successful in life.
5. What does the teacher want us to do?
The teacher wants us to finish this lesson.
6. What do students expect their teachers to do?
Students expect their teachers to help them learn.

Tape Script—Lesson 13

B. Listening, Reading, and Answering Questions

1. What has the president urged that the American people do?
   The president has urged that Americans save energy in a number of ways.
2. What has he suggested that people do to keep warm?
   He has suggested that people wear extra clothing to keep warm.
3. Has the president directed that the gasoline tax be lowered?
   No, he has directed that the gasoline tax be raised.
4. How has he proposed that people get to work?
   He has proposed that people form car pools to get to work.
5. What has the president advised that people do about water?
   The president has advised that people not waste water.
6. What has he insisted that Congress do?
   He has insisted that Congress pass an energy program.

C.
1. Why is it important that the student talk to her adviser early? in order to plan her schedule
   It's important that the student talk to her adviser early in order to plan her schedule.
2. Why is it vital that people save energy? in order to conserve it for the future
   It's vital that people save energy in order to conserve it for the future.
3. What is urgent that John do today? deliver the message to the director
   It's urgent that John deliver the message to the director today.
4. What is preferable that Mary not know until next week? the results of the exam
   It is preferable that Mary not know the results of the exam until next week.

Let's Practice IV—Verbs Followed by a Noun and a Gerund and Verbs Followed by a Noun with a Preposition and a Gerund

A.
1. What animal did you see climbing the tree? a cat
   I saw a cat climbing the tree.
2. What insect did Mary feel biting her? a mosquito
   Mary felt a mosquito biting her.
3. What did you watch flying in the sky? birds
   I watched birds flying in the sky.
4. What did you see swimming in the water? fish
   I saw fish swimming in the water.
5. What animal did you hear meowing? a cat
   I heard a cat meowing.

B.
1. What should they apologize for? being late
   They should apologize for being late.
2. What can't they talk their boss into doing? giving them a raise
   They can't talk their boss into giving them a raise.
3. What can't we stop him from doing? sending us flowers
   We can't stop him from sending us flowers.
4. What did the flu prevent you from doing? going out of town
   The flu prevented me from going out of town.

Tape Script—Lesson 13

C. Planning a Trip

> Yesterday when I finished doing my work, I decided to call my friend, Pete. Pete and I enjoy getting together for a drink once in a while, so I invited him to come over. We started to discuss our summer plans and agreed to spend some time traveling together. I had been thinking about taking my Volkswagen camper and driving to New England. Pete also wanted to see New Brunswick and Nova Scotia, Canada, and talked me into changing our itinerary quite a bit.
>
> "We'll have to count on being away for at least a month," I said. "Will your boss object to your taking so much time away from work?"
>
> "I don't think so," replied Pete. "He can't stop me from choosing my vacation dates. I have a month's vacation coming."

Questions

1. What did you finish doing yesterday?
   I finished doing my work.
2. Who did you decide to call?
   I decided to call my friend, Pete.
3. What did the two of you begin discussing?
   We began discussing our summer plans.
4. Where had you been wanting to go during the summer?
   I had been wanting to go to New England.
5. What did Pete talk you into?
   Pete talked me into changing our itinerary and going to New Brunswick and Nova Scotia.
6. How long will you have to count on being away?
   We'll have to count on being away for at least a month.
7. How much vacation time does Pete have coming?
   He has a month's vacation coming.

D. Dictation

1. Mr. Williams had the carpenter build a garage for him.
2. Traveling to other countries helps you to see how other people live.
3. Did you talk your boss into giving you a raise?
4. We saw the dog run across the street.
5. I reminded Jack to meet us at seven.

End of lesson 13

Lesson 14: Sports and Recreation

Conversation

1. What is John doing?
   John is sailing a boat.
2. What are Mary and Mike doing?
   Mary and Mike are dancing.
3. What is the Smith family doing?
   The Smith family is camping.
4. Who is ice skating?
   Sally is ice skating.
5. Who's playing tennis?
   Gary and Myra are playing tennis.
6. Who's playing baseball?
   Linda and José are playing baseball.

Vocabulary Focus

Sports and Recreational Activities

1.
   1. go swimming
   2. go skiing
   3. go waterskiing
   4. go scuba diving
   5. go sailing
   6. go canoeing
   7. go fishing
   8. go hunting
   9. go camping
   10. go backpacking
   11. go hiking
   12. go horseback riding
   13. go roller-skating
   14. go ice-skating
   15. go bowling
   16. go dancing
   17. go shopping
   18. Many Americans go camping in the summer.
   19. They go hiking and backpacking in the mountains.
   20. Do you want to go swimming this afternoon?
   21. I usually go shopping every Saturday.

2.
   1. play tennis
   2. play golf
   3. play football
   4. play soccer
   5. play volleyball
   6. play hockey
   7. play baseball
   8. play basketball
   9. play table tennis
   10. play cards
   11. play poker
   12. play bridge
   13. play pool
   14. play a game
   15. Let's go play tennis this afternoon.
   16. Let's go play basketball.
   17. Let's go play soccer.
   18. Let's go play cards.

Let's Practice I—Expressions of Preference: *Would Rather*, *Prefer*, and *Like Better*

A. 1. fishing or swimming
   Would you rather go fishing or swimming?
   swimming
   I'd rather go swimming.

Tape Script—Lesson 14

    2. waterskiing or sailing
       Would you rather go waterskiing or sailing?
       sailing
       I'd rather go sailing.

    3. soccer or hockey
       Would you rather play soccer or hockey?
       soccer
       I'd rather play soccer.

    4. basketball or baseball
       Would you rather play basketball or baseball?
       baseball
       I'd rather play baseball.

    5. ice-skating or skiing
       Would you rather go ice-skating or skiing?
       skiing
       I'd rather go skiing.

B. 1. I prefer to swim in a pool than to swim in the ocean. How about you?
       I prefer to swim in the ocean.
   2. Which do you prefer, living in the country or the city?
       I prefer living in the city.
   3. I prefer dogs to cats. What about you?
       I prefer cats to dogs.
   4. Which do you prefer, cooking or washing dishes?
       I prefer cooking.

C. 1. Which do you like better, soccer or baseball?
       I like soccer better.
       Not me. I prefer baseball.

       Questions: Which game does the boy like better? Which game does the girl like better?
                       The boy likes baseball better and the girl likes soccer better.

   2. Let's go fishing today.
       No, I don't like fishing very much.
       What do you like better?
       I prefer to go hiking in the woods.

       Questions: What does the boy suggest doing? What does the girl prefer to do?
                       The boy suggests going fishing. The girl prefers to go hiking in the woods.

   3. Do you like to play cards?
       Yes, especially poker.
       Oh, I like bridge better than poker.

       Question: Which game does the girl like better, poker or bridge?
                      The girl likes bridge better.

Tape Script—Lesson 14

Let's Practice II—Verbs with Inseparable Particles, Verbs with Separable Particles, and Verbs Plus a Preposition

A. 1. go in
       Let's go in this restaurant.
    2. go out
       John went out without his umbrella.
    3. start off
       We started off about nine this morning.
    4. stand up
       Don't stand up when you eat.
    5. sit down
       Please sit down in this chair.
    6. come over
       Why don't you come over this evening?
    7. turn around
       Bob turned around and saw Tim.
    8. go away
       Go away and don't come back.

B. 1. Dr. Smith hung up his coat.
       Dr. Smith hung his coat up.
    2. The child opened up the box.
       The child opened the box up.
    3. Frank wouldn't turn down his stereo.
       Frank wouldn't turn his stereo down.
    4. Lucy filled out the registration form.
       Lucy filled the registration form out.
    5. The class read over the lesson.
       The class read the lesson over.
    6. Please put out your cigarette.
       Please put your cigarette out.

C. 1. Hank's mother said, "Pull up the shades."
       But he didn't pull them up.
    2. Hank's mother said, "Turn off the light."
       But he didn't turn it off.
    3. Hank's mother said, "Put away your clothes."
       But he didn't put them away.
    4. Hank's mother said, "Don't wake up your baby brother."
       But he woke him up.
    5. Hank's mother said, "Don't take off your jacket."
       But he took it off.
    6. Hank's mother said, "Clean up your room."
       But he didn't clean it up.

D. *Example:* at

    1. to
    2. on
    3. for
    4. about
    5. of
    6. on
    7. after
    8. through
    9. for
    10. of

Tape Script—Lesson 14

E.
1. We were looking for the lost boy.
   We were looking for him.
2. John was looking at a book.
   John was looking at it.
3. We asked for the waitress.
   We asked for her.
4. We listened to the weather report.
   We listened to it.
5. Mr. Jones paid for the typewriter.
   Mr. Jones paid for it.
6. I thought of Tom yesterday.
   I thought of him yesterday.

F.
1. I filled out the form.
   I filled it out.
2. They asked for his opinion.
   They asked for it.
3. We opened up the bottle.
   We opened it up.
4. Grandmother will help take care of the children.
   Grandmother will help take care of them.
5. I'll call up George next week.
   I'll call him up next week.
6. I have to put away my things.
   I have to put them away.
7. We might call on our friends.
   We might call on them.
8. Did you think of your father?
   Did you think of him?

Let's Practice III—Expressions of Cause and Effect and Expressions of Contrast

A.
1. Mr. Carter lost the election. He didn't receive enough votes.
   Mr. Carter lost the election because he didn't receive enough votes.
2. Lucy had a bad cold. She didn't go to school yesterday.
   Because Lucy had a bad cold, she didn't go to school yesterday.
3. Jack dropped his Russian course. It was too hard.
   Jack dropped his Russian course because it was too hard.
4. I wasn't very hungry. I didn't want any lunch.
   Because I wasn't very hungry, I didn't want any lunch.
5. Our team lost the game. It hadn't practiced enough.
   Our team lost the game because it hadn't practiced enough.
6. We got there early. We had time for a drink.
   Because we got there early, we had time for a drink.

B.
1. We won't have school tomorrow because it's a holiday.
   We won't have school tomorrow because of the holiday.
2. Because there was an accident, everyone had to get off the road.
   Because of the accident, everyone had to get off the road.
3. Because there was heavy fog, the airport was closed.
   Because of the heavy fog, the airport was closed.
4. Our house was destroyed because there had been a fire.
   Our house was destroyed because of the fire.
5. Because it was raining, we had to postpone the picnic.
   Because of the rain, we had to postpone the picnic.

Tape Script—Lesson 14

C. *Example:* since

1. Since
2. since
3. as
4. as
5. because of
6. Because

D. 1. Mountain climbing is a popular sport although it can be very dangerous. a. F b. T
2. We enjoyed the camping trip in spite of all the mosquitos. a. T b. T
3. Carl went to Sweden because his mother lives there. a. F b. T
4. In spite of reports of a blizzard, we headed north. a. F b. T
5. Kevin used to go to Silver Lake every summer because of the good fishing. a. F b. T
6. Mr. Hawthorne enjoys life, but he isn't rich. a. T b. F

E. 1. Superior National Forest is well known because of *all its canoe trails that run through streams and lakes for hundreds of miles*.
2. People go canoeing in Superior National Forest in spite of *the possibility of bad weather*.
3. The American Indians made canoes because *they needed them for transportation*.
4. The French fur traders used canoes because of *their convenience*.
5. Canoes used to be made out of trees, although today *they are made out of lightweight materials, such as aluminum*.

Let's Practice IV—Result Clauses and *Whether Or Not*

A. 1. What is so small that you can't see it without a microscope? a single body cell
   A single body cell is so small that you can't see it without a microscope.
2. What is so far away that you can't see it without a telescope? the rings of Saturn
   The rings of Saturn are so far away that you can't see them without a telescope.
3. What is such a high temperature that water will boil? one hundred degrees celsius
   One hundred degrees celsius is such a high temperature that water will boil.
4. What is such a low temperature that water will freeze? zero degree celsius
   Zero degree celsius is such a low temperature that water will freeze.

B. 1. Will you write a letter even if you don't feel like it?
   I will write a letter whether or not I feel like it.
2. Will you buy some flowers if you have time?
   I will buy some flowers whether or not I have time.
3. Will José come by plane if he's afraid of flying?
   José will come by plane whether or not he's afraid of flying.
4. Can Marvin understand Spanish when people speak fast?
   Marvin can understand Spanish whether or not people speak fast.
5. Will you go to school if you are tired?
   I will go to school whether or not I am tired.
6. Can you finish your work if Mary helps you?
   I can finish my work whether or not Mary helps me.

C. **Dictation**

1. Do you know whether or not the students have made their vacation plans yet?
2. It was such awful weather last Saturday that we couldn't go on our picnic.
3. Bob was so tired last night that he didn't study for his test.

End of lesson 14

Lesson 15: Education and Future Plans

Conversation

A. **The End of Summer**

Nancy: I don't want summer to end.
Beth: Neither do I.
Nancy: I can't believe that school starts again in less than a week.
Beth: The time has gone so quickly that I haven't done half the things I had planned to. I wish we had at least two more weeks off.
Nancy: Nevertheless, you did have a chance to travel during the vacation. I was too broke to go anywhere. I'm worried about paying my tuition bills this semester.
Beth: I am too. Unless I get a part-time job in the fall to supplement my scholarship, I won't be able to afford to stay in school. Inflation is really terrible these days.
Nancy: I know. I can't keep up with it.

B. **After Graduation from College**

Mrs. Baker: What do you plan to do after you graduate, Kathy?
Kathy: I've always wanted to be an architect and design houses. I'll be a graduate student in the School of Architecture.
Mrs. Baker: How about you, Jerry?
Jerry: I plan to take business courses. I hope to be accepted in an M.B.A. program.
Mrs. Baker: And you, Patty?
Patty: I'm interested in making pottery. My dream is to set up my own ceramics studio some day. My uncle who lives in the country has an empty old barn on his land. I would love to have it renovated and converted to a workshop.

Vocabulary Focus

Educational Institutions in the United States

1. early childhood education or preschool
2. nursery school
3. kindergarten
4. elementary education
5. elementary school or grade school
6. secondary education
7. middle school or junior high school
8. high school
9. higher education
10. college
11. university
12. junior college or community college
13. technical schools
14. professional schools
15. special education
16. adult education

Tape Script—Lesson 15

Let's Practice I—Expressions with Verbs and Adjectives That Take Particles and/or Prepositions

A.   1. make up for
       You must make up for the days you missed from work.
       You must make up for them.
    2. run out of
       I ran out of sugar and had to buy more at the grocery store.
       I ran out of it.
    3. run out on
       After ten years of marriage, the man ran out on his wife and children.
       He ran out on them.
    4. try out for
       I tried out for a part in the play.
       I tried out for it.
    5. brush up on
       If you plan to travel to France, you should brush up on your French.
    6. catch on to
       Frank caught on to algebra very fast.
       He caught on to it.

B.   1. Mr. Marvin abandoned his wife and five children.
       Mr. Marvin ran out on his wife and five children.
    2. Will you visit us sometime?
       Will you drop in on us sometime?
    3. I used up all my money in Las Vegas.
       I ran out of money in Las Vegas.
    4. Did you understand algebra easily when you were a student?
       Did you catch on to algebra easily when you were a student?
    5. I have to review my notes before the test.
       I have to brush up on my notes before the test.
    6. They auditioned for the school play last week.
       They tried out for the school play last week.
    7. Did Mr. Smith ever regain the time he lost when he was sick?
       Did Mr. Smith ever catch up on the time he lost when he was sick?

C.   1. Bob wrote a letter to Mary. Mary received the letter.
    2. Bob wrote a letter for Mary. Bob wrote the letter instead of Mary.
    3. Bob mailed a letter to Mary. Mary received the letter.
    4. Bob mailed a letter for Mary. Bob mailed the letter instead of Mary.
    5. Mr. Smith sold a car to Mrs. Clark. Mrs. Clark bought the car.
    6. Mr. Smith sold a car for Mrs. Clark. Mrs. Clark owned the car and someone else bought it.

D.   1. A secretary types letters for the boss.   a. T   b. F
    2. My father paid the rent for me while I was a student.   a. F   b. T
    3. Mrs. Atkins taught an accounting class to three other teachers.   a. F   b. T
    4. John sold his bike to Alan.   a. T   b. F

E.   1. The boy was angry. his sister
       The boy was angry at his sister.
    2. Mr. Jones was proud. his children
       Mr. Jones was proud of his children.
    3. Susan was worried. passing the course
       Susan was worried about passing the course.
    4. Dave had grown bored. school
       Dave had grown bored with school.

Tape Script—Lesson 15

    5. Children are dependent. their parents
       Children are dependent on their parents.
    6. Richard was interested. making a lot of money
       Richard was interested in making a lot of money.
    7. They were opposed. our plan
       They were opposed to our plan.
    8. Brian is tired. traveling so much
       Brian is tired of traveling so much.

F. 1. Why was the child ashamed of his behavior?
       He thought his mother would be disappointed in him.
    2. Why did Linda teach the class for Julie?
       Because Julie was sick.
    3. Do you ever run out of money?
       I sure do. I run out of money at the end of every month.
    4. Who did the real estate agent sell the house for?
       She sold the house for my grandparents.
    5. Who did the real estate agent sell the house to?
       She sold the house to Mr. and Mrs. Foster.
    6. What is Peter afraid of?
       He's afraid of snakes.

Let's Practice II—The Verb *Wish*

A. 1. Whom do you wish to see tomorrow? my adviser
       I wish to see my adviser tomorrow.
    2. Where do you wish to go next year? New York
       I wish to go to New York next year.
    3. Why do you wish to learn English? study at a North American university
       I wish to learn English so that I can study at a North American university.
    4. What time do you wish to go home today? about five o'clock
       I wish to go home about five o'clock today.
    5. What do you wish you could do right now? play soccer
       I wish I could play soccer right now.
    6. What do you wish you could eat right now? a pizza
       I wish I could eat a pizza right now.
    7. Where do you wish you were right now? back home
       I wish I were back home right now.
    8. Do you wish you had a lot of money? Yes
       Yes, I wish I had a lot of money.

B. 1. Mr. Martin drives recklessly. What does his wife wish?
       She wishes her husband drove carefully.
    2. We're going on a picnic tomorrow and it will probably rain. What do you wish?
       I wish it wouldn't rain.
    3. Paul loves Mary but Mary doesn't love Paul. What does Paul wish?
       He wishes Mary loved him.
    4. They can't come next week. What do you wish?
       I wish they could come next week.

Tape Script—Lesson 15

C. 1. I don't feel well now.
       I wish I did.
    2. My feet hurt.
       I wish they didn't.
    3. I can't see you today.
       I wish I could.
    4. We have to take an exam later.
       I wish we didn't.
    5. Mark can't come with us.
       I wish he could.
    6. They will leave tomorrow.
       I wish they wouldn't.

D. 1. It's too bad Mary was feeling bad. good
       I wish Mary had been feeling good.
    2. It's too bad the patient died. lived
       I wish the patient had lived.
    3. It's too bad you misunderstood the directions. understood
       I wish you had understood the directions.
    4. It's too bad the books were old. new
       I wish the books had been new.
    5. It's too bad the post office was closed. open
       I wish the post office had been open.
    6. It's too bad the bus was running late yesterday. on time
       I wish the bus had been running on time yesterday.

E. 1. It was raining yesterday.
       I wish it hadn't been.
    2. Sam won't play tennis with us.
       I wish he would.
    3. The judge freed the prisoner.
       I wish he hadn't.
    4. The teacher will give us a hard exam.
       I wish he wouldn't.
    5. I can't sing very well.
       I wish I could.
    6. Bill doesn't like me.
       I wish he did.

F. 1. You plan to take a vacation next month. What do you hope? the weather will be good
       I hope the weather will be good.
    2. You're looking for a used car. What do you hope? can find a good deal
       I hope I can find a good deal.
    3. You want to go to the movies with Mary tonight? What do you hope? she will be free
       I hope she will be free.
    4. You intend to buy a camera. What do you hope? it isn't too expensive
       I hope it isn't too expensive.
    5. Your friend played in a tennis tournament. What do you hope? he won the tournament
       I hope he won the tournament.
    6. Your friend just bought a gift for you. What do you hope? he didn't spend too much money
       I hope he didn't spend too much money.

Tape Script—Lesson 15

Let's Practice III—Present and Past Participles as Adjectives and Past Participles as Adjective Complement after the Direct Object

A. 1. The trip was tiring.
       I was tired.
    2. The circus was exciting.
       I was excited.
    3. The movie was depressing.
       I was depressed.
    4. The weather was disappointing.
       I was disappointed.
    5. His strength was amazing.
       I was amazed.
    6. The magician was convincing.
       I was convinced.
    7. The speech wasn't interesting.
       I wasn't interested.
    8. The wild animals were frightening.
       I was frightened.

B. *Example:* boring (bored)

    1. The news that I received from home was (depressing) depressed.

    2. I felt   depressing (depressed.)

    3. Barbara was   interesting (interested) in biology.

    4. The biology lectures were (interesting)   interested.

    5. Foreigners are often   amazing (amazed) at some of the customs of this country.

    6. Listening to tapes in the language laboratory becomes (tiring) tired.

C. 1. We want someone to paint the house brown.
       We want the house painted brown.
    2. They are going to have someone do the work.
       They are going to have the work done.
    3. She wants to keep the window open.
       She wants the window kept open.
    4. We got someone to change the tire.
       We got the tire changed.

D. 1. How long did it take you to get your suitcase packed? half an hour
       It took me half an hour to get my suitcase packed.
    2. How long did it take Lynn to get the package wrapped? only a few minutes
       It took Lynn only a few minutes to get the package wrapped.
    3. How long did it take Jenny to have her hair cut? about twenty minutes
       It took Jenny about twenty minutes to have her hair cut.
    4. How long did it take the Smiths to have their house built? nine months
       It took the Smiths nine months to have their house built.

Tape Script—Lesson 15

Let's Practice IV—The Passive Voice (Part 2) and Sentence Connectors: *Moreover, However, Therefore*

A. *Example:* saw   were seen

   1. have received   has been received
   2. will discontinue   will be discontinued
   3. hadn't told   hadn't been told
   4. are helping   are being helped

B. 1. Was everyone asked to come on time? Yes
       Yes, everyone was asked to come on time.
    2. Could the work be done another time? Yes
       Yes, the work could be done another time.
    3. Are the results of the exam going to be published? No
       No, the results of the exam aren't going to be published.
    4. Does the car have to be washed? No
       No, the car doesn't have to be washed.

C. **Dictation**

   1. Jerry has a bad cold; therefore he shouldn't go to school today.
   2. College is important for most people. On the other hand, it is not necessary for everyone.
   3. Jane had a math test this morning. However she didn't study for it last night.
   4. Bill's car needed a brake job; moreover it had bad tires.

End of lesson 15